Your Business Your Future?

If you want to own a business like my wife does with **Teepees4kids,** (cover) which has customers worldwide, buy **Your Business Your Future?** to get going. It shows you how to go about it and why starting a business can be cheaper and safer than buying a used one or a franchise.

The author is a retired United Nations business development consultant and CEO of a household-name company, founder of two successful small businesses and a get-you-going business mentor. If you are thinking of buying a business, read **Your Business Your Future?** beforehand to see if starting one could be your best option and how to go about buying one if that is what you prefer

Also by Robin Rainbow

Published books:

Get Paid (CreateSpace, 2009) (Kindle edition, 2011)

Get Paid Painlessly (Reed Publishing, 2004)

Published papers:

Consulting for International Aid Agencies, 1998 *(Management Magazine)*

Complete Deregulation of the Philippine Motor Industry, 1997 *(United Nations Development Programme (UNDP))*

Motor Vehicle Taxation Reform *(UNDP & International Monetary Fund)*

Malawi/Zambia Glass Sand Development Scheme, 1985 *(UNDP)*

Business operating manuals:

Accounts Receivable Solutions (Australia), 2006

Accounts Receivable Solutions (New Zealand), 1988 and 2010

Internal Audit Manuals for the Stansfield Group of Companies (1978)

Your Business Your Future?

ISBN-13: 978-1516895892
ISBN-10: 1516895894

The Kindle version book number is B013VZGI2O

by

Robin Rainbow

Disclaimer. Going into business is not for everyone and whilst this book helps you do so it cannot guarantee or imply success as this very much depends on you. Also, as legal bumf such as tax, business and company structures vary between countries, states or provinces and like other aspects of business changes occur, readers are responsible for complying with local, state, provincial and national laws and all other requirements.

Your Business Your Future

Table of Contents

1_____Get going

Starting a business can be easier, cheaper and safer than buying a used one. It's also more fun (chapter 3). If you want to run-your-own-show this book tells you about everything you need to know, such as choosing the name (getting that right saves heaps and increases the resale value), setting-up, raising the cash and how to avoid having a tyrant for a boss when you are the boss ...

Why follow a seller's meanderings?

Starting a business stimulates creative thinking. Buying one either kills it or robs you of the cash to turn good ideas into, well, a business.

Creative thinking helps you to discover better ways of doing things, sometimes without spending a cent. So instead of buying a second-hand business use the money saved to develop the next big thing in your field, such as (write your ideas in the margins)

Going into business - alone or with others – gives you the potential to become one of the greats who have pioneered everything from inventing bows and arrows to pocket calculators*. These greats are called *entrepreneurs*. There is another group called *intrepreneurs* and some of these shine like stars too. But even if your name and photo never appear in the media, you can still be successful by creating something that brings employment to others and enjoyment (and money) to you.

* Clive Sinclair (UK) invented the world's first pocket electronic calculator, the *Sinclair Executive* in 1972

Begin by finding out what your business profile is because starting a business is not for everyone. This is because there are three types of personality* when it comes to starting or buying a business - ***entrepreneur, intrepreneur*** and ***employee.***

Entrepreneurs are independent. They want to own their business (or enough of it to influence its direction) with the freedom to make decisions and implement them. Successful entrepreneurs assess risk and take viable ones without worrying too much as they have plans B and C if things don't work out. They enjoy challenges others find frightening and are innovative, resourceful and are either very good employers or very bad ones – if they are bad their businesses suffer as shown later.

If you think you are an entrepreneur (or could become one) then starting a business is usually your best option. This is because entrepreneurs prefer inventing their own wheels instead of turning someone else's. But if you do buy a business avoid buying a franchise because knowledgeable franchisors don't like entrepreneurs because they cause trouble by tinkering with the franchisor's wheels.

Intrepreneurs are people who prefer having things already setup rather than having to invent them. Intrepreneurs can work for themselves but are more suited to buying a business with existing systems and a customer base. Good franchisors (avoid those who are so keen to grab your money they will appoint anyone who can pay) prefer intrepreneurs as they are less prone to rebelling. But you never own a franchise - you only rent it for a while, plus you have to adhere to the franchisor's rules otherwise they can terminate the agreement without refund. But before buying any business use this book to see if your intrepreneur traits can be turned into entrepreneurial ones. Achieve that and you won't need to buy someone else's overpriced business.

Employee. Starting a business can frighten people with an Employee Personality because there are no existing structures, rules or defined tasks. These have to be created as-you-go which is fresh air to entrepreneurs, but if it sounds daunting get help on how to make it fresh air for you and this book helps you do it. Buying a business can be daunting too, because whilst everything may be in place being the boss can be frightening

* Source: *Wareham's Basic Business Types* by John Wareham, CEO of head-hunters Wareham Associates.

and lonely. There's nothing wrong with people with Employee Personalities because most folk possess it – without them nobody would be happy working for someone else, which is clearly not the case. People with Employee Personalities can become intrepreneurs or even entrepreneurs but may not want to, in which case remaining as an employee may be best. Getting a job with a growth company headed by an entrepreneur could be ideal because Employee Personalities are valuable assets to them for many positions - perhaps including that of successor when it's time for them to bow-out.

Get going now

As well as avoiding shelling-out cash, starting a business can be less risky than buying one because risks are often downplayed - or not mentioned at all - by vendors. Risk exists whether you buy a business or start one but are easier to identify in the *what-if* stage when planning to start one because you will not be subjected to vendor propaganda. By identifying risks you can assess if they are acceptable – you may even find ways to change risk into opportunity.

If you start a business you avoid getting so bogged down running a bought one there isn't much time, or money, to develop anything new. You also avoid the risk of paying too much by relying on information and accounts provided by vendors - and paying for professional advice to verify it - then later discovering things are not as rosy as made out, yet without being deceived to the extent you can get your money back. If this happens you have a problem, so why take the risk?

Then there's the **Fun Factor** in starting your own show. This is an often overlooked ingredient of success and by creating it you will be inspired. So get going now because you can do a lot of it without spending money or quitting your job. Even if it seems that lots of money is needed, you might not need piles of cash to get going as shown in the *Raising the cash* chapter.

When going into business, age and background doesn't matter much because you can create and run a business if you know enough about the sector you are entering. If you do, whether it's window cleaning or perpetual motion machine making, shrug-off comments such as: *"it's too risky; you don't have enough money; you don't have......"* and so on. Instead of put-downs, look at what you have got - such as skills, energy, vision and write them in the margin because these can outweigh stuff spoilsports hurl around.

Investigating starting your own business right away helps prevent *if-only* attacks. This starts with: *"If-only I had the courage; If-only I had the money; If-only I had......".* *If-only* is one of the loneliest feelings in the world and attacks those who have made the wrong decision, made no decision or made it too late. Whilst it can be better to have tried and failed than to have never tried at all (but preferably not in business), test things out beforehand to reduce the risk

By investigating starting your own business now you will prevent *if-only* attacks. This starts with: *"If-only I had the courage; If-only I had the money; If-only I had......".* *If-only* is perhaps the loneliest feeling in the world and attacks those who have made the wrong decision, made no decision or made it too late. Whilst it can be better (but preferably not in business) to have tried and failed than to have never tried at all, test things out beforehand to reduce the risk.

The first *if-only* to avoid is: *"If-only I had the time."* Time poverty can be self-created because saying, *"I'm busy,"* sounds energetic when it can mean time is used poorly. Busyness is destructive if it turns the mundane into priorities that delay action on really important stuff until, say, tomorrow. That's like the bar owner who said, *"free beer tomorrow"* and when customers complained about the lack of it the following day replied, *"tomorrow never comes."*

Overcoming the *if-only I had the time* obstacle solves other delay issues, so complete the **Time Poverty Solver** over the page because "if-only" attacks bite long after reasons for busyness have been forgotten.

Time Poverty Solver

1 Who or what really controls my time? Me? YES ☐ No ☐ If No, who or what ....

....

....

2 If I ticked No in 1, How can I get rid of it? ....

....

....

When will I get rid of it? Today ☐ Later ☐ - if later, when? ....insert date because more than a month = never

3 What really motivates me? ....

4 What do I most like doing? ....

5 What do I least like doing? ....

6 What are my present priorities? ....

7 What are my real priorities? ....

8 Do the answers to 6 and 7 differ ? Lots ☐ Some ☐ Hardly at all ☐
   If they differ, this is what I will do ....

....

.and I will start on .... (date) and finish by ....

If it cannot be done in this time, will I ever do it? YES ☐ No ☐ (Be very honest to avoid a future 'if only')

9 How many hours a week do I work on average? Include commuting time .... hours

10 Do I work weekends? Lots ☐ Some ☐ Hardly at all ☐. If lots or some, why? ....

....

and do I take days off in lieu ? YES ☐ No ☐ If No, why not?............................

....

Continued on next page

11 Does my job/other people rob me of spare time Lots ❐ Some ❐ Hardly at all ❐ If

lots or some, why? ....

....

....

12 Do I now think I suffer from time poverty? YES ❐ No ❐ If YES the reasons are ....

....

....

and this is how and when I will fix them ....

....

....

13 If I answered YES to 12 I am vulnerable to 'if only' attacks   YES ❐ No ❐

Can I accept this now? YES ❐ No ❐ If YES, will I still accept it in 10 years time?

YES ❐ No ❐ If NO this is what I will do NOW to prevent it ....

....

Overcoming time poverty gives you the time to start planning your soon-to-be business. Start now because thinking is not action and without action the only thing likely to happen is, *if-only*. To inoculate yourself, check the worksheet daily (yes, daily – if you don't have time you really do have a problem) and using a green pen (I was an auditor until I grew up and green ticks mean everything's OK) tick the obstacles you have overcome until you can answer *NO* **to question 12.**

2____ Myths and facts of starting a business

Overcome those who want to choke your genius by stopping you from starting a business! Begin with a bit of relativity by separating myth from fact.

.

Einstein wasn't taken seriously initially.
(courtesy of physics.about.com)

The 'I wouldn't if I were you' myth

If you have a job you could be vulnerable to comments such as: *If I were you I would stay there as you are getting paid and the job is reasonably secure even though you are working for a bunch of ...*

Unless you are unemployed, your pay might be at risk if you start a business (it might not so read on) because you have to get customers and perhaps buy inventory, a vehicle and obtain premises. Or will you? If you do the groundwork before going into business, you could start earning straightaway. Whilst it's prudent to plan for a reduced income for around a year - some advisers say two years or more, but in that case, why bother to go into business? With sound planning you could reach, or exceed, your present income well within a year and *The Cunning plan* and *Raising the cash* chapter's help you work out how.

Now to the job is 'reasonably secure' bit of the *I wouldn't if I were you* myth. If *reasonable* means mediocre and you want more than that, look for another job or go into business. Very little is secure these days and few of us have any control over the booting-out time. You, and perhaps your employer, may never know when a receiver will walk in and fire you on the spot. Even a CEO is not immune because they too are only as good as their last results – I was a CEO for 15 years and was never fired, or asked to jump.

Risk myth

You risk losing everything if you go into business. What about your retirement fund? What about your car, your medical policy, life insurance and what-about the what-about ...

The Risk Myth thrives on fear, so cut the bogeymen down to size. Of course you may lose things when you leave your job, but sound planning can show if your business will be profitable enough to compensate. Use this book to work out whether the risks are just myths or if they really are threats that could destroy more than you can afford to lose.

One thing which is not a myth is the fact – and it is a fact – that if you have a spouse or other intimate who is not happy about you going into business, don't do it until you have fixed their concerns. This means really fixing them and not sidestepping or overriding them. Even if they are risk-averse by nature, they have reasons for it so take them seriously. After all you married/got-together for serious reasons, didn't you?

Grindstone myth

You *will never have a spare moment. You will work seventy hours a week, seven days a week including Christmas day.*

Be willing to put in long hours if needed, but only for a month or two. Even then, try and work only five days a week because all work and no play turns Jack and Jill into very dull folk. Long hours tend to reduce efficiency, so it takes longer to achieve less.

Aim for a forty hour week, or less, and whilst it's OK to exceed it occasionally, if you can't do everything needed (check if it really is needed) in forty hours something's wrong. If there is too much work, can you outsource it or employ someone? If outsourcing isn't possible and you can't afford to employ staff then look for an as-and-when-required contractor. There are probably suitable people in your neighbourhood, such as those with small children, the retired or semi-retired who would be delighted with casual work. Stick a notice on the supermarket noticeboard and see what happens.

If you're overworked but can't afford either option, find out why. Are overheads too high, customers not paying, are you under/over charging, paying too much for supplies or other reasons? This book helps avoid them.

Failure myth

If you fail you'll lose everything.

As with all great myths, the failure one is based on half-truths which can be as persuasive as full-truths. An example of half-truths is statistics showing that around 70% of new businesses fail. But, as the 19th century British Prime Minister Benjamin Disraeli said: "There are three kinds of lies: lies, damned lies, and statistics."

The **Reasons for not buying a business or a franchise** chapter shows that new business failure rate statistics are misleading. Of course some new businesses fail, but so do existing ones, including franchises (perhaps the one you are thinking about buying?). The supposedly high failure risk of new start-ups is a reason why many advisers say it's safer to buy a franchise or an existing business than it is to start one. But buying a business, or a franchise, is risky too – it's also costly.

Mortgage and other debt

Debt trap

If you are in debt, then debt is a fact and not a myth. Debt can stop or delay you from going into business because it will be serious if your earnings fail to cover living expenses and debt servicing.

(Illustration supplied by chanteepps.com)

But if you really have found a cash cow to milk right now, get going right now! If not, it's risky to leave your job if it means you can't pay your way because of an income drop that starting a business can – but not necessarily – involves. If you have large debts, hesitate before going into business until you reduce them, unless you are out of work and can't get a job. But if you can't get a job, think twice before going into business if the main reason for it is to buy a job. Thinking twice means achieving a mind-shift from that of an *employee* to *intrepreneur*, or even to an *entrepreneur*. Reading on helps achieve a mind-shift – when you do it could be the beginning of a new life.

Work out the risks

To separate risk from myth, use the ***Risk Action Plan*** (**RAP**) on the next two pages and the **Success Index Calculator** in the *Cunning plan* chapter. If you are married, or in a long-term relationship then both of you do the RAP - you might get some pleasant surprises!

Risk Action Plan (RAP)

1. Am I married?   YES   ☐   No   ☐   If YES, what does my spouse think about me starting a business? ....

....

2. Do I have a family to support? YES   ☐   No   ☐   If YES what **real** harm could they suffer? ....

....

3. Do I have any debts? (mortgage, credit card, other)   YES   ☐   No   ☐   If YES how will I service them? ....

....

4. Am I really suited to owning a business? YES   ☐   No   ☐   and why do I believe this? (before answering read chapter 3) ....

....

5. What do I really stand to lose?

    5.1 Family home YES   ☐   No   ☐ If YES where would I/we live? ....

....

    5.2 Marriage breakdown YES   ☐   No   ☐   If YES reassess the wisdom of going into business ....

....

    5.3 Job security YES ☐ No ☐ If YES what are the consequences? ....

....

    5.4 Salary loss   YES   ☐   No ☐ If YES what are the consequences? ....

....

....

Continued on next page

5.5 Pension & other benefits YES ☐ No ☐ If YES what are the consequences? ....

....

....

and If I go into business will I recover these with one year? YES ☐ No ☐ Reasons ...

....

....

6. What do I really stand to gain by starting my own business? ....

....

....

7. What things can I and my family can do without for a year?.............................

....

8. What are my goals and ambitions? (those which are sensibly achievable) ....

....

.9. What are my strengths? ....

....

10. What are my weaknesses ....

....

11. What do I now plan to do?
    a. Plan how to start my own business   YES ☐ No ☐ Maybe ☐

    b. Buy a business   or franchise   YES ☐ No ☐ Maybe ☐

    c. Look at all business options   YES ☐ No ☐ Maybe ☐

    d. Go back to work and forget it   YES ☐ No ☐ Maybe ☐

Why have I made this decision?...

....

....

....

3___ The fun-factor

If it looks like fun, steam ahead…

The fun-factor is more important to success than stodgy gurus and professors realize. When combined with sound planning and common sense (that's also often overlooked) they can make going into business the best thing you have ever done

The fun-factor is not hedonism. It's about motivation and happiness for yourself, your family, employees, customers, suppliers and others who will benefit from your refreshing attitude! Making business fun helps you succeed and letting the fun continue can increase the value of your business and make it easier to sell because the atmosphere will be attractive - and that's great fun for you and the buyer.

Work out ways of making your business fun. Start by finding out what motivates you because fun and motivation can influence your success more than qualifications. When people enjoy what they are doing they are motivated to do it well and in business that gives you a big advantage.

After over forty years in business I believe fun is more important than money provided you are earning enough to make it worthwhile. I have had the privilege of working with talented people on four continents that enjoy what they do to such an extent that happiness radiates from them. Such people are inspiring because their energy and enthusiasm are great for morale which makes employees enjoy their jobs. I have seen highly successful people encouraging staff, customers and others to get the most out of life by putting lots into it. Some have become role models by encouraging *an if they can do it then so can I* attitude. A lot of them rarely work long hours as they seem to accomplish what is required without needing to. Unusual? No it's not because they can be seen at parent-teacher sessions, school sports events and on family holidays. You can tell those who possess the fun factor because their families have it too.

Put the fun factor into your business and when you employ people be a funny ha-ha boss and not a funny-peculiar one. You can do it without affecting discipline because staff will be motivated to work diligently, so there will be less need to tell 'em off.

The fun factor gives you a sound start because employees, customers, suppliers and others important to your success will both like and respect you. Being liked and respected is pretty rare but not that hard to achieve. Depending on what your business does, if you achieve it you could charge a more than your rivals (don't overdo it!) because customers can be willing to pay a bit more to deal with people they like and who do a good job. "Like" in business generates trust and trust generates business which helps reduces costs, such as advertising, and increases the value of your business – that's great fun.

If owning a business is for you – feeling excited is an indicator - and if it looks like being fun the chances of success are good provided you soundly organise your soon-to-be business, so do the Tick Tock Test over the page ….

The Tick Tock Test

The Tick Tock Test helps reveal what makes you tick and how to make being in business fun. If you answer YES to question 13 you're on the way …

But before starting your Tick Tock **first read the Guide after question 13**

Tick Tock Test

1. Stick-ability. Can you take knocks and bounce back?

   YES ❑ NO ❑ MAYBE ❑

2. Can you prioritize the use of your time? YES ❑ NO ❑ MAYBE ❑

3. How good are your selling skills?   GOOD ❑ OK ❑ POOR ❑

(cont'd next page)

---

4. When trying to persuade yourself and others are your reasons at least 90% fact and less than 10% bull?

YES ☐ MAYBE ☐ NO ☐

(If YES your 'convincibility index' is 90%, if MAYBE it is less than 50% ,if NO it is a dangerously low 10%)

5. Leadership. Can you easily delegate? YES ☐ NO ☐

6. Do you almost always (90% of the time) focus on the important?

YES ☐ NO ☐

7. Are you a good organizer?   YES ☐ NO ☐

8. Can you learn new tricks?   YES ☐ NO ☐

9. Have you enough experience in your sector to avoid pitfall?

YES ☐ NO ☐

10. Are you willing to take calculated risks?

YES ☐ NO ☐

11. Can you make decisions without procrastinating? (or not too often!)
YES ☐ NO ☐

12. Can you get on with most people?   YES ☐ NO ☐

13. Was doing the Tick Tock fun?   YES ☐ NO ☐

Guide:

Question 1 is 'Stick-ability'. This is about recovering from knocks and setbacks and common ones are covered in the 'Up and running' and 'Catastrophes' chapters. You would be a bit odd if you liked taking knocks, but if you can bounce back without losing much sleep, you can run a business.

Question 2 is about prioritizing your use of time by concentrating on the important because that improves effectiveness and profits. If this is a problem, the 'Up and running' chapter or attending a Time Management course can fix it.

Question 3. If selling is not your strong point, don't fret because you can fix it later and doing so is fun.

Question 4. Your **Convincibility Index** concerns the ratio of facts to assumptions when attempting to convince yourself (and others) that your decision is sensible. If it is based on 90% being factual, the decision is very likely to be correct. If it is 50% the decisions is risky and risk increases rapidly after that. If the decision is made by only knowing 20% (or less) of the facts the odds are it will be wrong.

Question 5 covers leadership and self control. Whilst you might start as a one-man band and not need to lead others, you do have to lead yourself, and staff when your business grows. If leadership is currently a problem, it can be overcome by the experience gained from being in business, or by attending a one day leadership seminar.

Questions 6 and 7 are about focusing on the important and working out your priorities. Priority problems can sometimes be fixed by going for a walk, asking friends, colleagues or your spouse for advice, or by getting a decent nights sleep. Focusing on the important is tied up with time management and by fixing one you fix both. Doing so helps you to become a leader and organizer.

Question 8. The willingness to learn new tricks makes running a business more enjoyable – and profitable. By learning extra skills you reduce costs and improve effectiveness as shown in the 'Cunning plan' and 'Up and running' chapters.

Question 9. Knowing a lot about the industry or sector you intend to enter helps avoid pitfalls. The traps shown in the 'Hunting for a business' and 'Reasons for not buying a business or a franchise' chapters also help.

Question 10. The **Risk Index Calculator** in the *Cunning plan* chapter helps you assess risk. If risk frightens you, you are better off than those who play roulette as they may have something to be really frightened about. Yes, there are risks if you are in business, but you could also be run over by a bus, so work out the odds using your *convincibility index* score in question 4. People who use bull are also prone to using it on themselves, which increases the likelihood of taking unnecessary risks. If your score in question 4 is 90% or more you should be good at calculating risks and seeing if they are acceptable.

Question 11. Calculating risk in question 10 helps solve decision-making problems because it transforms fears into facts. Unlike most fears, facts are real which means most can be managed. If you calculate the chance of success is 80% you can identify the 20% risk element. Identifying risk puts it into proportion and doing that helps overcome procrastination. Whilst dithering occasionally can be prudent to avoid leading the Charge of the Light Brigade, if procrastination is a problem then by fixing points 2, 6, 7 and 9 procrastination can also be fixed.

Question 12 is about getting on with people which makes running a business easier. You may have to get on with people you don't like, such as prickly but important customers, key staff or fellow directors. Spitting out dummies at two is fine, but throwing tantrums at forty means damaged relationships and a poor performing business. It does not always mean divorce or bankruptcy, but it does reduce effectiveness as a business owner. This is because it's hard for such people to understand what drives others due to a, *what applies to me applies to you and if it doesn't there's something wrong with you,* attitude. This makes it difficult for them to work with others, and can be a reason why they want to work for themselves, but it is rare for their businesses to grow into sizable outfits. If they do, they risk being eased out by shareholders or partners because they create too many problems.

People with big egos can also be hard to get on with and whilst a big ego might not limit the growth of a business, it would grow much better without it because it doesn't impress staff and customers are not thrilled either. A simple way of finding out if ego is an issue is to ask someone, "Am I a big-headed know-all (or something) and if so, how can I fix it?" Those who daren't ask just might have a problem. If ego is a problem it can be fixed by a mind-shift, but if this proves hard it can be achieved by seeing a counsellor without having to tell anyone.

Question 13. Congratulations if you enjoyed the Tick Tock Test. If you did you probably scored highly! You might have scored highly without enjoying it, but isn't it more fun to do something enjoyable?

The Results – only read this AFTER you have done the test!

If you answered *YES, OK* or *MAYBE* to all the above, roll up your sleeves and get into business because it will be fun and successful if you plan it well. If you answered *NO* to 1, 4, 8, 9, 10, 11, 12 & 13 fix them before going into business using this book to help. You can overcome *NO* answers to the other questions with a bit of training.

4___Hunting for a business

Your green field's opportunity ...

If you have concrete-like ideas about buying a business, blow 'em apart because charging ahead without considering other options is like being a carthorse with blinkers on.

Starting a business stimulates big-picture thinking. You start with a clean slate and avoid inheriting small-picture issues that can become big problems the seller forgot to tell you about. After buying a business you then have to run it and become so entangled doing so that it spells the end of creativity. Even if it doesn't totally kill it, you might not have the money or time to develop something new, so the question then becomes: "Why did I buy it?"

Starting a business also lets you look at possibilities that advisors overlook - or downplay to avoid being sued by letting you step outside *their* comfort zones. This is what Thomas Jefferson, a major author of the Declaration of Independence and third president of the US, thought about advisors: "*State a case to a ploughman or a professor. The former will decide it as well or better than the latter because he has not been led astray by artificial rules.*"

Your proposed business may be related to your profession or trade, or do you want something new? For centuries entrepreneurs and adventurers have set sights on new things and whilst some have failed others have been spectacularly successful and have founded new industries. Whilst there are risks in going into the unknown, they can be managed.

A Lawyer's tale

Begin your journey for something new by looking at emerging sectors and those that are poorly serviced, like two adventurous lawyers did. They discovered that businesses selling on credit to other businesses (B2B is the jargon) had a need for debtor management seminars. These became so successful the firm became a leader in the getting-paid seminar trade, so they stopped doing ordinary legal work. If you are a surveyor, artisan – a lawyer – or about anything else, what have you or your rivals overlooked? Debtor management is not that far removed from the legal profession's core skills because law firms chase debtors and their seminars are spiced with creative ways of doing so without resorting to debt collection.

Start looking

Start your business-hunting expedition by updating your resume, but not as you would if looking for a job. Instead of emphasizing qualifications, experience and strong points, write down weak points because in a job you can sometimes disguise weaknesses, but when you own a business you can't. Identifying weaknesses helps you fix them and doing so overcomes a host of problems. Show your resume to somebody knowledgeable and ask them what they think you could do, and what you should avoid. But stay clear of negative types and only ask well-balanced ones. They don't need to be high fliers – keep Jefferson's ploughman and professor in mind.

Next, look at your skills to see what the opportunities could be because if a law firm can be entrepreneurial, so can you.

Refuse to pay a seller's dream price

Business author, Dr John Maxwell, wrote; *"At some point you have to make a transition from believer of the dream to buyer of it. No dream comes true without somebody paying for it."*

If you want to buy a business (or buy into one) only pay somebody's dream-price if it's really worth it. Few, if any, are worth it and the value to you may be much less when you consider the loss of opportunity you can suffer by buying it. If you really must buy it then ignore the fancy figures and other paraphernalia and only pay what its worth to you. Read the *Reasons for not buying a business or franchise* chapter before believing what a seller, his agent or accountant says about its value.

A little spadework

The law firm discovered their opportunity by helping clients recover bad debts. Unearth your hidden opportunities by doing some spadework - some (or all) can be done outside working hours. Start by looking at the Yellow Pages index (print version if they still exist) or go online to find sectors worth looking into which you hadn't thought of. Write down the interesting ones below so you don't forget, then compare them with your resume and your confidant's comments to get from the hunting phase to the shortlist stage.

My Spadework Opportunities are:

If you unearth a yet-to-be-developed sector, or a poorly serviced one, it could be the best investment in time you've ever made. Chuck out unsuitable sectors, plus those you could never get to like because entering a field you don't like isn't fun – but don't throw out sectors you could get to like, or could learn more about, because it would have been a big mistake for the law firm to have eliminated debtor management seminars. Complete the **Business Shortlist** on the next page to see what your likely options are.

Business Shortlist

1. Industries or sectors that I have identified are ....
....
....

2. If extra sills are needed, I can get them from ....
....

3. How long will it take to get the skills?.............. and it could cost $..............

4. What does my experience and resume show that I am good at? ....
....

5. What type of work do I like most? ....

6. What type of work do I like least? ....

7. What sectors in (1) are really suitable for me? ....
....

8. How well do I know the sectors in 7? A lot ○   Sufficient ○ Not much ○

9. What are my strengths? ....
....

10. What are my *REAL* weaknesses? ....
....

11. Is more research needed to identify new sectors or opportunities? If YES,
it is...
and this is when & how I will do it...
....

12. The start-my-own-business shortlist now is (only do this after finishing
your research in 11) ....
....

Question 12 eliminates unsuitable sectors to reduce the risk of failure because only having a little knowledge is dangerous to your wealth. If they really appeal you could start learning a lot about it.

The following helps prevent assumptions:

My sector knowledge is: excellent ☐ good enough ☐ not good enough.

Reasons for this are ………………...

Do I need to know more ? Yes ☐ No ☐ If YES how and when will I get it…

……………………………………………………………………………………………

What are the risks? …………………………………………………………………

……………………………………………………………………………………………

Can I afford the entry cost? Yes ☐ No ☐ If NO how will I raise the money?

……………………………………………………………………………………………

Cost of failure to me/my family is …………………………………………………

……………………………………………………………………………………………

Is the timing right? Yes ☐ No ☐ Reasons …………………………………

What assumptions am I making? …………………………………………………

……………………………………………………………………………………………

.

What is my next step? investigate further ☐ or abandon it and think again ☐

Reasons …………………………………………………………………………….....

………………………………………………………………………….........…......

Have you unearthed something that tickles your fancy? If *Yes* dig into it, but try and avoid early enthusiasm and assumptions steamrolling over your commence sense in case it won't work – better to find out now than later because the road to ruin is littered with ideas that haven't worked.

The good news is that you don't have to know everything to run a business. If you are a plumber you will know lots about plumbing but probably next-to-nothing about accounting, so forget the books and outsource your bookkeeping - and other things you find hard to do or don't like - and earn a living instead.

An academic failure

Avoid assumptions because they are dangerous. An old CEO told me that the road to ruin starts with an assumption. Two assumptions mean you're well on the way and three makes it a dead cert. He was dead right.

A business failure caused by an assumption is MENSA – a club for people with high IQs. The founder's obituary in *The Economist* (their obits reveal stuff you don't hear at funerals) said that MENSA was intended to be a business and a source of income for its gifted members, on the *assumption* they would sell their expertise to governments and corporations needing solutions to problems beyond the ability of mere mortals to solve. To fix them, all they had to do was phone MENSA. The phone never rang, so MENSA is only a club and not a business.

The ideal new business

The fairy-tale new business is one that is (or will be soon) in a growth area that is cheap to enter, has high profits and ongoing business from more and more customers! Whilst there aren't many yet-to-be-discovered sectors out there, you just might find one like another lawyer did.

A glamorous lawyer's tale

When starting a business, such as plumbing or law, it may sound hard to then jump into a glamour sector. But this is exactly what another lawyer did when he offered to totally manage the affairs of the then-aspiring golfer, Arnold Palmer. These included selecting sponsorship deals, tournaments to play in and other affairs beyond the normal expertise of lawyers. This business is now called the **International Management Group (IMG)** which claims to be (possibly rightfully) the global leader in managing the affairs of the world's glitterati.

It may be coincidence that two creative businesses were founded by lawyers, or perhaps it's because law, accounting (there has been some unfortunate creativity there) and other professions are not capital intensive to start. But capital is needed to buy an existing business, which brings about another creativity-destroying factor - justification. So as well as having no money or time to develop something new you have work the business to keep it viable, and to justify buying it. Why bother?

Even if you have clear ideas on which sector to enter, hold off and using the lawyers as an example hunt for something exciting. If you find it investigate it because you could make a fortune and have fun.

If your ideal business is so capital intensive you cannot raise the cash, then look for people with complementary talents to go into business with. This works if everyone is trustworthy, can work together and contribute capital – see the **Setting it up** chapter. For a very capital intensive sector you may never find the wherewithal to enter it, and even if you do it may not be a good idea. In that case look at entering the fringes; the profitable bits, the ones that are growing and do not need too much money to enter. To find out, use the *Capital Intensive Sectors* questionnaire below.

Capital Intensive Sectors

Capital intensive sectors that interest me are:

1 ....

2 ....

3 ....

3 Less capital intensive fringes I could enter are

1...

2 ....

3 ....

Advantages I have over existing competitors are ....

....

....

This is how I will I investigate starting up ....

....

....

What about outsourcing?

Outsourcing is the jargon for businesses (and governments) contracting out stuff they used to do themselves. Outsourcing is intended to improve efficiency, reduce costs and improve cashflow.

If your skills and experience can be used to help others reduce their costs and/or improve efficiency then you could start an outsourcing business. Possibilities include maintenance of plant and equipment, credit control and debtor management and a wide range of other activities, so jot down your options below.

My outsourcing possibilities are

Spying

To avoid an *if-only* attack and missing a life changing opportunity, investigate your possibilities with a bit of *Information Gathering* - sounds more upmarket than spying. Start by investigating the competition to see if there's enough business for you all. Then look at the national and the local economies and if it's good (or bad) nationally, will it be good (or bad) locally?

Every city, state and country has its prosperous and poor areas plus those in between so figure out which one yours is in and why and is it likely to change for better or worse.

I spy a lawyer

Giacomo Casanova (1725 to 1798) famous as a womanizer was also a spy for the Venetian State Inquisitors. He was also a lawyer.

His many affairs with powerful women made him powerful and very rich - it is said he gambled away the equivalent of $1 million in one night.

Industry/sector survey

How to spy depends on what you need to know and how much time you've got. If you are a *time poverty* sufferer you just might be tempted to think you already know all there is to know about robot washing machines – but if you don't you risk going broke when the things run amok. Investigating now also helps prevent future "if only" attacks if you ditch your plans because of lack of time to do your homework. As you've read this far at least find out if your ideas are a potential *wow* that could make you millions or a damp squid that could cost you your shirt or blouse.

Test your current knowledge or start your spying by asking yourself (or those who know a lot about the sector/industry) the questions overleaf:

If you need to ask other people you may need to undertake a survey so work out the best way to spy i.e. phone, email, post and if you should do it in your own name or pose as a student or researcher. Surveys involve samples so see the 'Statistical Significance of Samples' after the following Industry Survey questionnaire.

Industry Survey

1. How would you best describe the state of your industry?
Growing
Mature
Declining

2. What are the biggest threats to your industry ? ....

....

3. Who or what is the biggest threat to your company? ....

....

4. (a) Is the number of competitors increasing?
Yes ❒   **No** ❒   **Don't know** ❒

(b) What are the names any new entrants or departures? ....

....

5. If you had a choice would your firm remain in the industry and why? **Yes** ❒   **No** ❒
Reasons if YES ....

....

Reasons if NO ....

....

If NO what other industries would you switch to and why? ....

....

6. Other matters that are important to you (keep it as simple and as short as possible)

....

....
Persons name ....

Company ....

Statistical Significance of samples

Information gathering from top players and a few others is called *non-proportional stratified sampling* in academic-speak. To keep it simple, if there are 100 firms and you want 80-90% validity around ten firms at random need choosing. Random *must be random* and not just contacting those you feel like approaching. From your list of businesses select the first, the tenth, twentieth and so on. Whilst this is OK for a feasibility it is not very accurate, so if a serious survey is needed borrow a book on statistical sampling, or buy lunch for somebody who knows how to do it.

No survey is perfect but you can learn enough to make a decision. So read the survey results like an outsider would to avoid catching rose-tinted-spectacle disease, which is easy to catch but results in your money getting the flu.

A dentist's tale

In case you think I have a fixation with lawyers, here's how my dentist friend got going. When I was in my early twenties I wanted adventure, so I went to Malawi (Africa) as a company accountant and befriended another adventurer, an American dentist at a mission hospital. He later went home and spied out modest size towns where he could start a practice and found a town with one long-in-the-tooth dentist who wanted to retire. Instead of buying the practice he started his own. My pal is an excellent dentist with a chair-side manner that charms patients' and the latest costly equipment. He got a second opinion on his plan, which was sound despite the huge debt for the equipment. The plan would have worked (but not as well) if the old dentist had managed to sell. He didn't as the town and rural surrounds were marginal for two dentists, so he retired.

My pal's practice flourished and before he got long-in-the-tooth he sold it to a young dentist who would have had problems setting up in a town with a rival with a good reputation. Buying a business can be the best way of going into business, but this shows how well you can do by starting one then selling it.

Having a long lasting monopoly is unusual, but if you can find one that is hard for others to challenge, get going right now before someone else does.

Write your advantages down

Before starting or buying a business, write down your or its competitive advantages using the form on the next page and the reasons for them. If the advantages are not being used by rivals, find out why - has nobody thought of them, or have they been tried and failed? If they failed, why will they work now? Another reason for writing them down is to help remember the best potential ones, because potential becomes money when it becomes real.

Competitive advantages:

Competitive advantages are:

1

2

3

...... and more if you have them

4. Why are they competitive advantages? ………………………………………...

………………………………………………………………………………………..

………………………………………………………………………………………..

5. Have they been used before, did they succeed? YES ❒ NO ❒ and why …

………………………………………………………………………………………..

………………………………………………………………………………………..

6. Are they still being used? YES ❒ NO ❒ If YES, why can I use them as well as or better than my rivals? ……………………………………………………..

………………………………………………………………………………………..

7. If NO, why can I successfully use them now?………………………………….

………………………………………………………………………………………

8. Will I have a monopoly. If yes, how long will it last and why? ……………..

……………………………………………………………… *Cont'd next page*

....

9. Have I invented or discovered a totally new concept or product? If YES,

what ....

....

10. Who will be my customers?...

11. Why will they be my customers?...

....

12. Why will I succeed in this business?.......................................

....

....

Whilst you probably will know who the competitors are, what you are unlikely to know is; who else is about to enter? If demand is growing others will pitch up so plan for it here:

Existing competitors are:

Who and/or how many other competitors are there likely to be?

Cont'd next page

How will I compete with them?

5_____A cunning plan

Will it take off and stay up?

To get fired-up about your soon-to-be business, write a farewell speech to your workmates on why you will be a millionaire in a month. If you are going into competition with your employer tell them you are starting a laundry – you sort of are and they may be the first wash.

The speech isn't a joke - it's the start of a business plan and by making it fun you are more likely to complete it, and for it to be read by those you need to read it. Whilst it is a bit unusual to be a millionaire in a month, your business should be prospering in less than a year. The reason for treating your plan as a speech at this point is because you are compiling a half page summary of what your business is about.

"But I know window cleaning inside out and don't need to borrow money, so why write a plan nobody will see?" OK, but will you clean home, shop, office, factory windows or the lot? You don't need to write anything fancy, but something formal helps get a loan for the ladders or convince an investor to put their money in. It can also help you sell the business when the time comes, which is covered later. Even if you don't need to borrow money, going into business without a plan is as risky as going to sea in a small boat with your family but without charts, life jackets, water, adequate clothing or checking the weather forecast.

Avoid revealing your secrets in the summary, so if you are starting a laundry, don't disclose the ingredients of the washing powder that will make the competition look dull. Only disclose confidential information to outsiders on a strict need-to-know basis, and if they don't need to know don't tell 'em. If you have to disclose secrets, insist they sign a confidentiality agreement beforehand - see **Appendices** for an example.

Compile a title page (below) for your cunning plan, but as it will become important to the success of your business, call it a 'Business Plan'.

Business Plan

Len's Laundry
(to be incorporated)
123 Washwhite Street, Sudsville
Tel 3999 1700
www.washwhite.com
Email len@washwhite.com

Follow the title page with a table of contents and modify it to suit your business.

Contents

Overview
Reasons for starting the business
Market situation & Competitors
Marketing plan
Sales plan
Budget and finance
Investment
Share capital
Plant, equipment, vehicles
Premises and fit-out
Start-up
Opinions of qualified persons

The plan needs to be just long enough to show that the business is viable – first to you then to bankers or others. You can do all or most of it yourself, or if an accountant is needed by doing as much as possible reduces the fee.

If your plan has to be shown to others, making it look good can get them to read it. Whilst it's quality of content that counts, enter *business plan template* online to get a feel of presentation styles. Try to include a few pictures because, as the saying goes, "a picture is worth a thousand words." That's why brochures and prospectuses look pretty, even if the product or investment is ghastly. But don't overdo it as dignity outweighs razzmatazz because you are writing it for bankers and the like who prefer facts and not fiction.

Looks can woo them

Around 80% of business plans are rejected by bankers and most others in the first few minutes (I can't recall where I got this data from but it came from a credible source) so improve the odds by making yours well-written and plausible by avoiding comments such as, *there are no competitors and everyone will buy it.*

Overview

The good news is you have already done this – it's the summary compiled from your farewell speech.

Reasons for starting the business

The main reason for writing down why you are starting-up is so *you* know the reasons This helps you to be objective and if you are happy with the reasons then you can confidently tell others who need know. Even if you don't need to borrow money, having your plan assessed by a capable outsider can save problems if key elements have been omitted or there are unrealistic assumptions, such as rags to riches overnight.

Show why the business will succeed and what's required to achieve it, but avoid divulging the ingredients of your washing powder and the blueprints of your robotic washing and ironing machines. State why you are capable of starting the business by including your qualifications, experience and other things that make you appropriate for it – be frank to avoid deceiving yourself.

In your reasons for starting the business include a SWOT - **S**trengths, **W**eaknesses, **O**pportunities and **T**hreats. Whilst SWOT has been around for years it's not old hat because it works, provided it's done carefully. It's fun doing a SWOT, especially if the results excite you. The following is the SWOT for Len's Laundry - Len was a real person who started what became a British household-name company but his name wasn't Len and it wasn't a laundry - but there's nothing wrong with laundering as long as it is clothes and not money.

- *Strengths*: superb knowledge of laundries, superior washing powder, inventor of robotic washing and ironing machines (patents pending);

- *Weaknesses*: lots of competitors, lack of money, risk that new inventions do not work;

- *Opportunities*: Can seize a sizeable market share with robotic washing and ironing machines and whiter than white washing powder to knock the socks off rivals;

- *Threats*: Washing powder doesn't work, laundry market shrinks.

Market situation

Another reason why many business plans are rejected is they paint rosy pictures and ignore threats. If everything really is rosy, explain why it will remain so and what could take the shine off. Show the current situation of the laundering industry; such as businesses paying staff laundering allowances for doing it themselves. If possible prove (including to yourself) how your equivalent of robotic washing machines will send old fashioned laundries to the cleaners. Work out the likelihood of your robot rebelling and just why it will work, without revealing the secrets, then state how it could fail but without frightening yourself to death and killing a good idea. If you know the industry well you

can estimate the risk of failure – but to be positive call it a
Success Index as shown below.

Success Index Calculator

Success & Risk	Odds	Reasons
Very high odds of success:	+90%	Robot has been thoroughly tested & demand for it thoroughly researched
High odds of success:	+85%	Robot well tested and sound reasons for good demand
Good odds of success:	+80%	Robot well tested with estimated demand
Acceptable odds of success:	+75%	Robot not totally tested yet no evidence of failure and with estimated demand
Borderline odds of success:	+66%	Robot not totally tested and has slight but fixable flaws
Risky:	50% to 65% certain	Robot partially tested with unfixed small flaws
High risk:	Less than 50% certain	Robot erratic and little market testing

Len fully tested his whiter-than-white washing powder
and it shines. But he doesn't expect the advantage to last long,
yet believes the robotic washing and ironing machines will give
him a sound advantage. He is also working on a perpetual
motion washer that uses no water or washing powder which
could attract Crowdfunding or Venture Capital investors to
transform the laundry into a major appliance maker.

Competitors

Every product and service has competitors. If you have a new invention the problem could be that nobody sees the benefit and won't buy it. But if it will benefit some of them, such as a baldness cure that really does work, it won't be long before you get a call from a huge pharmaceutical outfit wanting to buy you out. Until them you need to work out how to overcome customer reluctance to buy it which is covered in the Washing weekly chapter and needs including in you business plan.

Your investigations should have identified the competitors, what they are up to, why you can compete and where the industry is heading. If you haven't done this to at least a 75% confidence level do it to save your shirt or skirt and complete the box below.

Competitors and threats to my business are:

Competitors

Number of main competitors is ....

Number of minor competitors is ....

Write down the names of the main competitors

Write down the names of the minor competitors

Threats

Threats to the industry are ....

....

....

Cont'd next page

....

Threats from new invention could be ....

....

....

....

Marketing plan

Unless you are a doctor, dentist, accountant, or dare I say, a lawyer, if you intend to offer a service, such as software or other intangibles, market them as **products and not services.** This is because it's hard to create emotional appeal in customers for stuff they cannot drive, feel, cuddle or otherwise physically handle. This is what entrepreneur James Altucher, an author, fund manager and founder of several businesses says about marketing:

"If you are offering a service, call it a product. Oracle did. They claimed they had a database. If you bought their database they sent in a team of consultants to help you install the database to fit your needs. In other words, for the first several years of their existence, they claimed to have a product but they really were a consulting company. Don't forget this story. Products are valued higher than services."

It's not just customers you have to persuade to buy your product, you may need to convince bankers or others to put their money into your business. To do this your marketing plan and financial projections must be convincing. The following is what an opposition politician once said about the government of the day:

"You are like Columbus because when you set out you didn't know where you were going; when you got there you didn't know where you were and when you came back to your senses you didn't know where you'd been. And you did it all on borrowed money."

Columbus hadn't a clue where he was really going

If you do a Columbus the money will ultimately have to be repaid. But you are unlikely to get the money if the business plan is unsound and as the marketing plan forms the basis of the financial projections, avoid comments such as *everybody will buy this.* For a laundry, a bit more than *everyone needs to launder* is needed, so show why they will use your equivalent of a laundry and how you propose to get them as customers.

Your market plan can be magical and fun. The magic bit is it becomes a budget, cashflow and income and expense account to show you (and others) how profitable your venture will be. The fun bit is it can be your exit or retirement plan by providing an estimated value of your business when you want to launch it on the stock exchange, or sell it - this really is fun if it's worth heaps.

When writing your market plan you can discover what your competitors charge, what you can charge and what your costs are. So the marketing plan really is a cunning plan that kills heaps of birds with a pen or computer. Advertising comes into it too; especially how little you need spend, as covered in the *Washing Weekly* chapter.

Being in business should be fun, but it's not a joke, so your marketing plan needs to be at least 90% fact with less than 10% being assumptions *based on the factual 90%.* It would be nice for it all to be factual, but if you wait that long you will never get into business. The thing to avoid though is making it 10% fact and 90% bull because if you do your business might leave the ground using your initial funding as fuel, but will crash when it runs out.

Have a go at doing the marketing plan yourself. It saves heaps and can be as good as one compiled by a consultant. If you don't know how, enter *marketing plan* online. There are lots to choose from (good, average and dreadful) and some good stuff is free. The rest of this book will enable you to become a connoisseur on the good, bad and ugly and if you need paid-for help it helps you discern the good from the rest.

Forecasting sales/income

Forecasting involves a bit of guess-ology and getting it right is still as much of an art form as it is a science despite what some statisticians, software and other gurus claim.

As Groucho Marx reputably said, *"forecasting is hard, especially forecasting the future,"* but do your best.

Calculate realistic sales targets and not pie-in-the-sky stuff to avoid kidding yourself. Try to base it on 90% fact and show your sales, or income, by monthly steps for the first year and ideally for year two. If you can't find any facts (why can't you - is your sector so new there aren't any facts to base sales on?) you are in Groucho Marx Land which means a high risk of getting it wrong.

Groucho Marx, wit and comedian

If you are a dentist or window cleaner you should have an idea what other dentists and window cleaners earn. If not, look at the state of the premises where the surgeries of some of them are and their houses and cars or the state of other window cleaners' ladders, vehicle and homes.

When starting a business its hard to test sales forecasts beforehand but by writing them down you, or outsiders, can see if they are realistic. If you have got this far you will have the uncommon sense of checking things so that, bar catastrophes, you are more likely to succeed, which MENSA didn't.

Selling time

Businesses folk have one common bond regardless of whether they are painters, dentists, accountants, lawyers or retailers and that is they all sell time. Owners spend time in their businesses and what customers' buy pays for the time spent working in them. If you are a painter, your charges cover the time and materials - the latter are bought at trade price and sold at retail.

If your products are tangible goods you may be tempted to calculate selling prices by *cost-plus* (costs plus a mark-up). *Cost-plus* is old-fashioned and has been replaced by *pricing to the market,* which means charging what people will pay. You can make more (or less) this way so calculate your prices by spying on your competitors. If it turns out you can't make much of a profit there's no point in going into business, but better to find out now rather than later.

If your *products* are intangibles, such as Oracle's, or you will charge an hourly rate you may have the problem of customers objecting to your fees. To avoid, *"I'm not paying that much!"* it is common to disguise hourly rates. Audit fees are examples as these are usually a set fee and the client doesn't know the hourly rate. Vehicle workshop invoices often show the mechanics' hourly rate and vehicle manufacturers supply dealers with manuals showing the time needed for each job. If customers object they may be shown the manual as proof. But many jobs take less time than shown, so workshop productivity can be 120% to 150% or more. That means mechanics are paid for (say) a forty hour week but obtain 48 to 60 hours of chargeable time for their employers. Keeping hourly rates at a level that doesn't drive customers away, but charging more time than it takes happens.

Charging customers for idle time, lunch breaks or whatever is bad business. You just might antagonize them and when they find out they will go elsewhere. Collective sin by claiming everybody does it is unacceptable and someday a rival will stop doing it and that someday should be now and start with you. Then you can righteously pinch customers from overcharging rivals.

If you sell goods, customers are unlikely to know the mark-up. If you are a painter, it would be unwise to charge more than retail for paint because customers can check it. People often get quotations and you may not know what your rivals quote, so if you don't get the job ask why – was it price or something else? If you have superior quality, better features and are at the quality end of the market, you could charge more than your rivals. But be careful because customers might not value them attach as much as you do. So if your plan says you can charge more than customers will pay you risk going broke.

Budgets

Budgets are sort-of done by smoke and mirrors. There's no real mystery about them and if you can add two and two and make four you can be as good as those charging $150 or more an hour because they do the same. Keep 2+2=4 in mind so you don't make it whatever you want it to be. You know how little money you've got, which is a good start because poverty sharpens the mind.

On the basis you intend to throw money around like someone with no arms, do a zero-based budget. This means: *"If I don't need to spend it I won't spend it."* - it really is that simple. Zero-based budgeting is not new and remains popular because it works. Its basis is that the only reason to spend money is to make a profit; which means earning more than you spend, so when it comes to spending, start with zero.

Len's Laundry's zero budget is below - after reading What's-in-a name in Chapter 6 he renamed it *Industrial & Domestic Laundering* to get a higher price when he sells it.   The budget is **before** Len withdraws any money for himself - he avoids taking out all of it because his accountant said it would be prudent to keep some in reserve.

Len's Laundry (now Industrial, & Domestic Laundering (IDL)	
Budget: Year 1	
Sales	$990,000
Less: direct expenses	$520,000
Gross trading profit	$470,000
(47.5%)	
Expenses	
Rent	$ 48,000
Repairs and maintenance	$14,500
Advertising	$ 34,500
Vehicle expenses	$ 15,600
Admin salaries and wages	$ 78,000
Phones and postage	$ 7,200
Interest and bank charges	$ 12,000
Insurance	$ 6,000
Power and water	$ 14,400
Depreciation	$ 24,000
Staff refreshments	$ 3,900
Sundries	$ 6,000
Total expenses	$224,600
Net profit before proprietor's drawings	**$ 245,400**

Sales

Len's sales are based on people and businesses who said they will use his laundry. He has given them attractive introductory offers and is 75% certain that 75% of them will take up the offer and the 25% who won't can be obtained from people who come in once the doors are open (the jargon is *foot traffic*).

Direct costs

Direct costs are those incurred in running the laundry - wages, washing powder and everything else directly incurred in producing clean clothes. As Len knows how to launder, the gross trading profit of 47.5% is above the industry average of 40%.

Expenses

Len knows what the rent will be, but tried to avoid rent by working from home. Sadly, whilst working from home is fine for money laundering it isn't for the washing sort. Repairs and maintenance are estimates, but Len knows what equipment needs monthly servicing and what can go wrong. Advertising has been calculated using the *Washing Weekly* chapter and Len will ruthlessly say no to sales reps phoning about features in *Washing Weekly*; but in case one could be valuable he has a $3,000 contingency. Vehicle expenses are based on the number of kilometres needed to get new business, maintaining existing customer relationships plus collecting and delivering washing. He was tempted to put deliveries in Direct Costs but for better control has kept it separate. Admin salaries and wages are for those nice office ladies who do everything to keep the business running – especially credit control. Phones, postage, printing and stationery have been calculated on what is needed; insurance from quotations; depreciation from the nice little book the taxman kindly sent and interest is from the $120,000 loan needed to start the business. Staff refreshments are morale boosters and joining staff during breaks boosts if further as Len finds out what's really going on in the business, especially customer comments which otherwise he might not hear. Sundries are those minor odds-and-sods that will probably be incurred. Len decided against a 5% expenses contingency in the budget because it's arbitrary, but if worst-comes-to-worst the profit can stand it.

Cashflow

Cashflows are not done by smoke and mirrors - they are deadly serious because it's dead easy to underestimate the amount of cash needed. Just because sales are $82,000 a month doesn't mean this is what is being banked because if you are selling on credit, payment might only occur 45 to 60 days after the sale. At any one time you could be owed $120-164,000 which is why a cashflow is needed. Unless you know a lot about it, have your figures compiled, or at least checked by, an accountant or other experienced person. The following is Len's first year cashflow.

Cashflow

INCOME	Month	2	3	4	5	6	7
Opening Balance		(59750)	(79375)	(65125)	(48750)	(28750)	(8750)
Washing income	0	30000	64000	64000	64000	64000	64000
Ironing income	0	10125	18500	18500	18500	18500	18500
Nappy service	1250	1250	1250	1250	1250	1250	1250
Curtain service	1000	1000	1000	1000	1000	1000	1000
Other							
Total Income	2250	42375	82500	82500	82500	82500	82500
EXPENSES*							
Monthly expenses							
(from budget ÷ 12)	62000	62000	62000	62000	62000	62000	62000
Balance carried fwd	(59750)	(79375)	(65125)	(48750)	(28750)	(8750)	+9250
Taxation**							

*Taxation: Len will see an accountant as it's too important to leave out or get it wrong

Len's cashflow for year one is based on the budget and that business customers will be granted credit because the competitors do, so only the nappy and curtain services are cash sales, so washing and ironing income is nil for the first month.

If the cashflow shows instant riches falling out of the sky, the odds are it's pie in the sky, so look at the sales forecast again as this is where most get-rich-quick errors begin. Cashflows that reveal poverty can usually be trusted more than get-rich-quick ones. Next, look at expenses again to see if something essential - and expensive – has been omitted. Then put your miser hat on and eliminate things you can do without. A new car might be nice, but if your vehicle is a workhorse then buy, or lease, the ideal one for the job – one that does what you need it to do.

A vehicle, ladder, hose pipe and water blaster are essential if you are in the water blasting business, so you only need spotlights if working at night is part of your competitive advantage. If you have an office-based business, only have a suite on the 50th floor of Bankers Building when the cashflow justifies it. In the meantime, work somewhere more modest.

Only buy stuff when it's needed and not before. The only exception is (if you can afford and justify it) during periods of high inflation. When buying stuff, shop around for the best deals, but there is no point wasting time on deals for pencil sharpeners. Get three quotations for expensive stuff then ask for extra discount or other concession. If they are giving big cash discounts see if they will still give it for a deposit with the balance paid later. It's your money so don't be shy as their rivals up the road might give you credit and if you buy on the first day of the month you may only need to pay for it at the end of the following month.

If you cannot afford to pay-as-you-go for expensive and essential items, look at leasing them as there can be tax benefits, but shop around for the best lease deals.

A little matter of money

Your ideas might now be shaping-up but where's the money coming from? The 'Raising the cash' chapter helps find it and instead of making the bank your first port of call, make it your last.

If your business looks sound and profitable with good long term prospects but you are scratching your head about finding funds, take these words from Winston Churchill aboard: "Never give in, never give in, never, never, never, never: in nothing great or small, large or petty – never give in – unless it is to convictions of honour or good sense." So stick with it, continue with your plans and read on to help calculate how much working capital - or how little - is needed.

6_____ Setting it up

Get the name right before going for it hammer and tongs

The great news is you can do most things needed to set-up your business out of working hours. To get fired-up start by choosing the ideal name.

Selecting the right name is exciting and even better it lowers the amount needed to get going because a bulls-eye name can reduce advertising costs to little more than the cost of business cards.

What's in a name?

A lot … The right name saves heaps in advertising because it tells people what you do. If you are a lawyer specializing in injury claims, say so to differentiate you from other lawyers and if you are a window cleaner, do you clean all windows or do you specialize in shop, house or office windows? If so, state it in your business name. If you call your business *All Windows* (provided it's not a trademark of a software outfit), then instead of attracting everyone with windows, you might not attract anybody because there's little to differentiate you from the competition. If you clean all types of windows, say so – such as *Gem Window Cleaning: homes and commercial* – but if you specialize in high rise, warehouse and skylight windows then saying so will attract customers with those windows.

Before selecting a name, check that nobody else is using it. If your surname is McDonald you will have an interesting time if you call your sewage tank emptying service *McDonald's Takeaways* – it existed because years ago in New Zealand I saw their sludge tanker with *McDonald's Takeaways* written on the back end and BIG MAC as a personalized plate! Something may have happened since because they have disappeared. Another example was *Harrods Store* – a ramshackle shack on a side road near a volcano. If your surname is Deloitte and you are an accountant, you could have a bit of bother with another

Deloitte if you use that name. If you want to trade as Bluebird Pet Shop you possibly could, but if you intend to start a food business called Bluebird Foods you will encounter problems when the other Bluebird Foods finds out. Most countries also have restricted names that cannot be used for decency or national interest reasons - you could have an interesting time if you call your detective agency FBI, especially when you want a website.

Checking that the name will not cause problems saves money and time. If there is a future objection it will be costly because of name change, new stationery and signs etc. You can do the checking online for free to see if the name is available, or if it is a trademark or patent. If you don't know which government body handles business names and trade marks enter *intellectual property* or *restricted names* or *trade mark registry* into a search engine.

Using personal names for a business, such as Len's Laundry or law firm partners Sue, Grabbit & Runne is a disadvantage when you want to sell it because the buyer may want to change it. Whilst there are a few exceptions, such as the global accountancy firm Deloitte, personal names usually have no value to potential buyers. So instead of Len's Laundry, Len could change it to, say, *Industrial & Domestic Laundering (IDL)* or *Work & Injury Legal* for the law firm. But whatever name you chose, check that it cannot be confused with that of another business, trade mark or other restriction.

Have a bit of fun and Insert your name possibilities below:

My business name options
1
2
3
4

But before making a final decision read the **What's in a brand** section in *the Washing Weekly* chapter.

What to trade as?

The following varies from country to country and may change. The reader is fully responsible for checking and complying with their local/state/national legislation and other requirements.

Sole trader

If you operate as a sole trader you are personally liable for your business debts and all other claims and if you cannot pay you can be sued or bankrupted. It's as simple as that.

Being a sole trader though is a low-cost way of starting a business because providing the name is not already in use or protected, you can quickly get to work.

Trading as

If you are Peter Plumber but you trade as *All Plumbing* you are still personally liable for all debts and liabilities of *All Plumbing* in the same way a sole trader is.

Partnership

A partnership is two or more people in business together. But it's risky to be a partner as each partner is normally jointly and severally liable for the partnership's liabilities. Generally, any or all of the partners can be sued and if one cannot pay the others have to. Even if you totally trust the person(s) you are in business with, forming a partnership is not a good choice as you are all vulnerable to legal action. However, *limited liability partnerships* are possible in some jurisdictions and are popular with some professional people.

Limited liability company

When going into business seriously consider forming a limited liability company. You can form a company anytime but if you leave it until after starting-up you may be too busy to get round to it and you will have to change your stationery, so do it beforehand.

The shareholders (stockholders in USA) of a limited liability company cannot usually be sued unless it is for the unpaid portion of share capital. To solve this, start with a low nominal share capital of say $1,000 (can be $1) and pay it up-front. Whilst directors and other office holders can be personally sued in some circumstances keeping your nose clean reduces the risk, but seek advice from a lawyer or accountant on this. You can form a company yourself but if you are unsure about it see an accountant or lawyer.

Commonly used company jargon is:

Directors
The boss/bosses but only one is needed in many countries.

Shareholders
Those who put the money in – it can be one person, a trust or another business (in USA shareholders are stockholders).

Share capital
The amount of money going to be put in.

Paid up capital
The amount actually paid – if not all of it is paid upfront the balance is still owing.

Call
This is a demand to pay some or all of the unpaid share capital. It can occur at an inconvenient time and could be made by a bank, receiver or liquidator.

Constitution
This is what the business and directors can or cannot do.

Minutes
Bits of paper showing what has been agreed at directors or shareholder meetings. They sometimes show what should have been said and not what was actually said!

Annual General
This is to appoint directors, auditors (or not to appoint any) and other stuff.

Debenture/charges Bits of paper given to somebody (often a bank) saying they have a priority claim on the company's assets. In Australia, Canada, New Zealand and other countries, property securities registerers have replaced most traditional charge documents.

Tax

More than a passing interest is taken by government on paying taxes and whilst you cannot ignore it on the basis it will go away you don't have to tackle it yet. But do so before you start trading either online to the tax website or ask an accountant.

Trademarks and patents

If you checked the registers during the name search you may be surprised at what can be registered as trademarks and how crass some are! You may want to register one and spending time on the official websites could enable you to do-it-yourself. That save s heaps.

The advantage of protecting intellectual property with a trademark is it stops others from using the name (if you will be trading internationally, get legal advice). It's not too hard to register a trademark yourself but patents are more complicated and a lawyer is normally needed. Patent attorney fees can be high and patents can be risky because formulae or full details of the products have to be disclosed, which gives competitors an A to Z how-to. This is why some businesses avoid taking out patents and instead rely on the complexities of their inventions for protection. If you have a new and innovative product or concept on which patent protection could be desirable seek legal advice. Avoid letting details enter the 'public domain', which basically means it cannot be patented and anybody can use it. Public domain can include publishing information anywhere, so avoid blogs or otherwise letting details of it be known.

Other

Setting up a business is usually straightforward and can be done cheaply in a few days, or less, in most developed English speaking countries. However, if yours will be a complicated business, such as mining which individuals sometimes do in Australia, Canada and elsewhere you will probably need professional advice.

7_____ Where to work from and other stuff

When he's not out-and-about it's good enough for James Bond, but does it suit you?

Put that nice name you chose on hold and call your business *Miser & Co* for the time being. This makes it easier to keep your moneybag tightly closed to see how little they need to spend. A starting point is slashing rentals to bits.

Rent-avoidance is another advantage of starting a business. If you buy one, odds are it will operate from premises and is geared up to continue doing so. "But I'm starting (buying) a wholesale/retail business and am bound to need premises." Why? I know an office stationery owner who runs it from his garage. Instead of carrying lots of inventory (stock) he keeps as little as possible and orders as required. He also imports stationery and keeps it in a storage warehouse (they now sniffily like being called *logistics* companies) and by shopping around he got a cheap rate as there are lots of them. The rent and cashflow savings by having minimal stocks means he can undercut competitors and still make a tidy profit. When the time comes for him to sell, the buyer can operate the business from his own garage. Doing this with a bought business with large inventories and premises is hard.

If a stationer can do it you possibly can too, but check if there are zoning restrictions, especially if you will be doing anything noisy or industrial. It may be illegal, and unfair on your neighbours, if you have presses thumping away day and night. If you are storing materials in your garage, ensure you comply with regulations and your insurer's requirements.

Drive around to see how many home-operated businesses there are. Many have their business name on the fence and are likely to include accountants, lawyers (of course), other professionals, plumbers, electricians, wholesalers and many more.

If you live in rented premises, the landlord's permission will be needed for business use. Ask your insurers too because their approval is needed for activities of a non-domestic nature conducted from home. If you have not told them and have a claim it could be rejected, so think of the consequences of the loss of your home – and business - caused by your undisclosed activities. Depending upon what you do depends on whether there will be a premium increase. If it is a desk-based business where your equipment is a computer there may not be, apart for the extra premium for your equipment.

Tell your insurers if you will be using your vehicle for business because if you have an incident or it is stolen they can reject the claim if you were using it for business at the time. There will probably be a premium increase but better safe than sorry.

Working from home impresses customers if your prices are lower than the competition, but if price reductions are not necessary think what that will do for your profit! It's easier to work from home if customers rarely need to visit you, but even if they do, lower prices in exchange for sitting in your study, garage or shed can offset it, so keep your miser hat on because slashing overheads is fun, and profitable.

A Home Office

This is a home office in a wardrobe - the doors are shut when the office is closed. It is in the home of a rep of a large pharmaceutical company as big firms also let staff work from home.

This is the home office of a state sales manager of a pharmaceutical company. It is a built-in wardrobe and the doors are shut when the office is closed. If a corporate encourages it, can you do it too?

For self-discipline it helps to have a regular starting time and you are *at work* from then on.

There can be tax savings by working from home because some household costs are deductible including a percentage of rates/property taxes, phone, electricity, other outgoings and the cost of work related alterations. But speak to an accountant first because in some jurisdictions there are capital gains or other tax problems arising from a home being used for business. A family chat beforehand can solve domestic issues before they arise, such as where do the children play. Chores are another reason why your spouse's cooperation is needed because hanging out the washing, answering domestic phone calls and the like makes the home-worker vulnerable to distractions. Ask them to remind you – and you remind them - that whilst you are working from home you are not *at* home. Showing them the benefits, such as the extra money available for eating out or going on holiday just might help.

Stuff you need and stuff you don't

Phones: Do you really need a landline phone or will a smart phone do? If a landline and directory listing bring in business then get them, but some businesses have ditched landlines. So the question is, *do I need a landline?*

Faxes are becoming outdated, but if customers order or send vital documents by fax then instead of buying a fax, look at getting a virtual one. You can then send and receive faxes from your computer or phone from almost anywhere, so enter *"email fax"* on a search engine to see if it will work for you.

Furniture – unless you need fancy furniture to impress customers and bring in business then to save money can you modify furniture to serve as a desk or bench? If you are sitting down a lot one thing not to skimp on is a decent chair because you will spend a lot of time on it and getting a good one will improve efficiency, comfort and can save you from back problems. There may be other equipment you would like but can't afford, such as a photocopier or a lathe. In that case, go to a copy centre or outsource your machining and if the volumes are high, ask for a decent discount. If you need expensive equipment, or vehicles, instead of buying them look at leasing.

Leasing v buying

There are two views on leasing. One is that leasing is more expensive than buying because lease companies make their profit from the rentals (of course they do otherwise they wouldn't do it) and receive discounts from the equipment providers. They also make a profit on the resale of the equipment if it is an *operating lease* (one where the equipment remains their property and is returned on expiry of the lease). Some agreements give you the option of buying the asset at a reasonable price on termination.

The other view is that leasing can be cheaper than buying because lessors negotiate better prices with suppliers and give some of the savings to lessees. If you are short of cash, or can more profitably use it in your business, leasing is attractive but unless you are familiar with leasing see an accountant first as there can be a fishhooks.

Renting

If you really must have premises avoid being pressured into signing anything before getting advice from a lawyer or accountant. Things to be wary of are zoning restrictions on what can be undertaken as you could end up with premises you cannot use, and a lease you can't get out of. Other issues are the length of the lease and right of renewal. You should have the right to renew, but not be forced to (be wary of this risk) and if the premises turn out to be unsuitable later – especially if you outgrow them – a sublease clause is needed. You can then find a tenant and if you are cheeky you might make a profit by charging a higher rent. Most leases contain a clause requiring the landlord's prior approval for sub-lease in case the new tenant is undesirable, but permission must not be unreasonably withheld.

Check that the rent is fair by asking other tenants, or occupiers of neighbouring premises - they may tell you if you are not competing with them. Then there are rent revues, so negotiate these if they are loaded in the landlord's favour, which they are. Most leases contain a clause stating that the rent will never come down and may rise at every rent review date. These are called *ratchet clauses* so try and get them deleted because if there is an oversupply of premises in future better deals can be had. A ratchet clause prevents this and whilst you might not succeed in getting it deleted try and negotiate something more favourable.

Also, what about rates/property tax, electricity and other charges? Are these levied or are they included in the rent? Rates usually are but power rarely is, so ensure that the power bills are not loaded with an admin charge and the ideal is a separate meter in your name so that you only pay for what you use.

Copyright © 2012 Sony Pictures

See what the lease says about fires, floods and anything else that can make the premises unusable, so check what will happen if disaster strikes. If you have seen *Skyfall* you will have some idea of what can happen and you don't want to pay the rent if it does. Look for other fishhooks and what insurance is needed. A trip to your lawyer could be a sound investment after all.

Starting-up

Planning your start-up date can get you fired up and whilst it would be nice to have everything tied up beforehand it might not work like that, so if there are a few loose ends don't lose sleep as you are no different to the majority of other entrepreneurs. Plan your start-up by setting priorities and dates, but be flexible as you will be lucky if nothing needs changing.

Start-up priorities

To do	Completion date
Completion of preliminary business plan	(date)
Completion of market research	(date)
Completion of sales plan	(date)
Final completion of budgets/cashflow	(date)
Finance options decided upon	(date)
Start-up procedures I can do before resigning	(date)
Provisional start-up date	(date)
Visit to chosen professional advisor(s)	(date)
Review by advisor(s) required by	(date)
Implementation of advisors recommendations	(date)
Finance options completed	(date)

Loan application approvals expected by	(date)
Investor/share capital funds needed by	(date)
Premises (if required) needed by	(date)
Capital equipment needed by	(date)
Stocks/inventory needed by	(date)
Final decision on whether to proceed	(date)
Resignation from job	(date)
Start-up	(date)
When to review progress	(date)

8_____Washing Weekly (advertising)

When Len thought about advertising Washing Weekly came to mind but apart from launderers the only other readers are DIY washaholics who are unlikely customers.

You can't cuddle an advert so spending money on it isn't fun, so cuddle your wallet or purse and keep it closed and find out what free advertising you can get because slashing advertising budgets to bits improves profits.

An advertising agent may ask you what you want to achieve with advertising. Before answering, ask them what they think advertising is about. According to David Ogilvy (founder of advertising agency Ogilvy & Mather) it is: *"to sell your goods or services because it has no other function worth mentioning."* His previous jobs were chef, farmer and spy.

Another question an advertising rep or agent will ask, and which you should never answer, is: "How big is your advertising budget?" If you tell them they will help you spend it all, so make your budget zero and as poverty sharpens the mind look at the free and cheap options. And cheap doesn't have to be nasty.

Free and low cost advertising

Word of mouth

The most effective media is word of mouth and it's free. It is effective because it's what people say about you instead of what you say about yourself. So no matter what your business is be nice to people; especially to those who could refer business to you. Be nice even if you have a monopoly and customers, clients or patients have no choice but to come to you because if you are not-nice, word of mouth will spread it around and it won't be long before somebody decides to do something about it, such as set up in competition.

Word of mouth carries weight as it is usually regarded as true and can stimulate instant action if the listener has a need. Odds are they will because word of mouth is selective - they wouldn't be told about you if it was of no interest to them. So before spending money on adverts that tell others about you, ask yourself *who could say good things about me?*

Social media

The effectiveness of social media depends on what you are selling and to who. If you want thousands of *friends* to buy your cosmetics be friends with everyone, but do you really want the hassles that can bring? Experiment because my wife's *teepees4kids* business gets good responses on Facebook free of charge. But to get a first page listing you usually have to pay which is what lots of businesses do when they say *follow us on ....book* or whatever. That means it's not free so social media is in the **Paying for it** section.

Existing customers

A slight downside of starting a business is you won't have any existing customers, but don't fret because your competitors do, so find out who they are. You might not be able to find out their names and addresses, but you can build a profile of the customers you want to attract. If you can identify some, ask them what would attract them to you.

If you buy a business you will inherit customers (if not, what are you buying?) so unless you are providing as-and-when-required services (such as a doctor and even then check-ups can be marketed) contact them to see if you can get them to buy more. Loyalty program are well established and are still used because they can work, so consider special offers to existing customers or a discount on the next purchase made within a month or so.

This is how I can attract my competitors' customers..................................

....

....

....

This is how I can attract repeat business from existing customers

....

....

....

....

Credibility

Credibility is delivering everything you promised and preferably a bit more than promised because that creates word-of-mouth referrals. If you have existing customers, then over-deliver by giving them something to increase their goodwill and your credibility. When starting a business you might not have any customers and not much credibility either, so see if others such as friends, customers of previous employers or anyone else can provide it. Try and get references and/or referrals from those you have helped in the past including the customers of previous employers and use them as free adverts, provided they agree.

Other businesses

You can get free advertising from other businesses if your products help their customers, so list those who could give you sales leads. If you only have a few contacts, or it is unwise to approach them, see who else could help. All of us buy from somebody – a vehicle workshop, hardware store and so on - so start with them and as you are their customer they are more likely to help. Even if they cannot help they may know people who could, so ask – it's free. If you are shy about asking it gets easier if you don't have much money. As the owner of *Miser & Co* do your best to overcome shyness because when going into business you have to get customers.

Try and form referral alliances with complementary businesses whose products dovetail with yours, Some alliances are obvious, such as lawyers and accountants and others with common linkage, such as similar customer bases. To form a referral alliance you need to offer something worthwhile then do your utmost to point referrals to them otherwise it will not work. It has to be reciprocal to endure.

These people/businesses could promote my business or form referral alliances

1

2

3

These are the benefits to them for doing so (examples only so insert yours):

    Mutual referrals

    Discounts on my products

    I will buy from them if they help me

    Other................

Networking

Networking is similar to referral alliances but broader. Informal networks can be persons from unrelated businesses who agree to pass leads to one another. Regular meetings, say working breakfasts, help forge relationships and to share information and a phone call or email can pass on leads. If you don't know of a networking group, start your own or join a formal one, such as those organized by a local business development body or look at joining the likes of Business Network International (BNI) – example only and not a recommendation.

Birds of a feather shouldn't stick together and good networks have diversified members ranging from lawyers to painters because leads can come from anybody. If you join a network, or start one, ensure that the membership is as broad as possible, but restrict it to only one from each trade or profession to avoid conflict of interest which will eventually break it apart, as will those who do not attend the breakfast or other meetings or are all take and no give. Join another network or kick them out if there are people like that.

The integrity of other members (and you!) is vital, so before joining a network, or inviting others to join yours, check they are not shysters or your reputation could be damaged, especially if you recommend them to your customers.

What's in a brand?

Brands are not just for corporates as small businesses can have them. Andrea Bean, Accountant, or Peter Plumber Plumbing says what Andrea and Peter do but in a dull way. If they called their ventures *Business Builder* and *Plumbers Around The Clock* these can become brands

(photo - the author's kitchen)

Our window cleaner has a brand which is also the trading name of his business, *Gem Windows*. His card has a twinkling diamond logo and so does his vehicle along with, *Gem Window Cleaning – homes, offices, factories, casual or contract* with his contact details.

He enjoys a good reputation and his charges are reasonable – not too dear but not cheap either - and he phones his non-contract customers when he believes their windows need cleaning. *Gem Windows* appeals to people's emotions far more than *Craig's Window Cleaning* ever will. When Craig decides to sell his business (which he started) *Gem Windows* has a customer base and a saleable brand. If he traded as Craig's Window Cleaning and sold it to Fred Smith, Fred would probably change the name to Fred's Window Cleaning so Craig would only have the customer base and ladders to sell and not the brand.

A brand is exciting and can be your competitive advantage which makes it an asset when its time to sell your business. So invent a brand name with emotional appeal to make you different from the competition. The jargon for this is *positioning* which is valuable because it sets you apart from the competition. If you are better than they are (or at least as good as) a reputable brand attracts new customers, can retain existing ones and just might enable you to charge a teeny-weenie bit more. *Positioning* though is determined by customers and not by the seller, so you need to work at it, such as giving superior service, better workmanship or by being nicer than the others.

By giving your brand a feel-good-factor *Miser & Co* won't need to spend as much money on advertising because the brand does it for free. So, instead of trading as Deirdre Deloitte, Chartered Accountant and if auditing is your specialization think about creating a brand, such as *Ten Cents A Tick Audits*. Well, perhaps not quite that, but you get the point.

Business card

Not any old card will do, so get one that says exactly what you do. Doing that turns a boring business card into an effective and cheap form of advertising!

I once attended a seminar where the presenter got everyone to lay their cards on the table to judge which was best. Some had glossy logos, others were printed portrait instead of landscape and one was oval. He said the best was from a freight forwarder as it showed exactly what they did. It was landscape, had only two colours and a small self-created logo in one corner. Mine was an also-ran. Annoying really as it had been designed by an *expert* whose expertise we then ceased using. The winning card fitted into a standard business cardholder, which are made for landscape cards, so portrait cards have to be viewed sideways which means they are easily overlooked. The oval card was worst as it wouldn't fit into a cardholder.

Become a card connoisseur to see which ones show what the business does and design yours so it shows what you do, then get opinions on it from business-folk and not from your grandma. A way of becoming a card connoisseur is to visit restaurants frequented by business-folk because some have bowls of cards by the till for draws for free lunches. If you ask nicely, they may let you peep at them if you tell them why and promise you won't take any. If they refuse then don't dine there. To be different, your card can also be used for a letterbox drop or scanned and turned into an email (avoid making it an attachment) and send it with or without a message – keep the message short i.e. *Could You Need a Plumber?*

Logo

Is a logo necessary? If you are a funeral director perhaps not, but some do have logos and nearly everyone else seems to have one. If you decide to have a logo (Gem Windows has one) then have a go at DIY like the freight company. If you are not arty some printers offer a free design service provided they do the printing.

If you have to pay someone, get a quotation – in my case getting a price was hard as the designer said "it depends". On asking why she looked me in they eye and said 'It depends on how many times you reject our ideas.' My reply was "Get it right first time and I won't reject it."

Over lunch the CEO of the Australian operations of an oil company said how much they had spent designing the logo that beams from their filling stations - you could start *a big* business for that amount. It was not just the money it was the time senior management had spent on it and the distraction caused them to lose market share. Recovering it and overspending their advertising budget reduced their profits which caused a bit of a stir at their annual meeting.

Stationery

Apart from business cards and an invoice/receipt book (off-the-shelf) our window cleaner has no other stationery. His main advertising is dropping business cards into mail boxes, membership of a networking group, a sign-written vehicle and making follow-up calls to get repeat business. I think this guy's a genius.

Work out what you really need and the odds are its far less than 10 years ago. You may or may not need letterheads or compliments slips and if only a few are needed run them off on your printer. For larger quantities professionally printed ones look nicer and to get a better deal, have business cards and (if it could increase sales) small telephone note pads that say what you do and have your contact details discreetly on them. Most of the pad should be blank so they can be used by those you give them to at their work, or even better at home as shopping jotters so they think of you when not at work!

Brochures/flyers

Do you really need brochures or flyers? If yes, who will receive them, will they be read and how will you send them – by direct/junk mail, placed on a counter or brochure rack? If you are a dentist, a picture of shiny teeth outshines your high-pitched drill. Pictures are best – people see them first – then as few words as possible. Brochures are costly if they are four colour and you may have seen cartons of out-of-date ones being thrown out. Do you really need the things?

Website

Gem Windows don't have a website. But Craig has email and a phone. So, do you need a website? Comments such as, *you don't exist if you don't have a website* are drearily negative and in the case of Gem Windows, untrue.

If you really need a website (the test is will it bring in business?) then get one but not because everyone's got one. Despite what gurus say, websites that do not have a click-here-to-buy-now option are really only electronic billboards. Even if they look pretty with all the gimmicks, getting them in #1 position on Google (or even the first page) is often costly.

Speaking

You don't need to be a Margaret Thatcher to get your message across (Photo by author from the cover of The Economist)

Speaking is easy as we have been doing it since around the age of two. It's also free advertising. If giving a speech frightens the daylights out of you, give a talk instead. Leave speaking to politicians as they love it, and the difference between a speech and a talk is in a speech the speaker is the centre of attraction (so they hope), whilst in a talk others are encouraged to interact or ask questions. Achieving this lets you promote your products and entertain people.

Almost anyone can be an entertaining guest speaker. You also get a free lunch or dinner. A talk on plumbing and how to overcome problems can be helpful and funny if you throw in some anecdotes - and they might call you when they have a problem. If you are an accountant, a talk about how to unearth the real truth in a prospectus or thrilling stories about frauds and tax audits can be entertaining and educational.

The only limitation to getting free exposure is a reluctance to give a 10 to 15 minute talk. Rotary, Lions and other clubs are often short of guest speakers and their members are mainly business people. Finish with, "I will be delighted to answer any questions after the meeting" and stay for awhile afterwards - give your business card to everyone who asks questions because the odds are they will have a need sooner or later. Some may want to know more, so ask for their cards and phone them later if others want to speak to you.

Daunted? Put your miser hat on and think about how much cost-free business you can get – and the free lunch. Decide what to talk about – it's fun and easier than you probably think. Preparation time for a 15 minute talk is 30 to 60 minutes, which is not long for a free lunch and for getting business you otherwise wouldn't get. I use four to six prompt cards made by folding A4 paper into four and cutting it (I prefer 120gsm as it's more robust than standard 80gsm). The prompts remind me of what I'm going to say and by rehearsing the talk all you need are prompts or a summary of anecdotes and you're in the talk circuit.

Writing

If you can read this you can also write! There's no magic to it because writing is similar to speaking - if you know what you are talking about you can also write about it. Whether you are writing letters, e-mails or articles you are doing it to sell your products and not to pass an exam, but do check spellings and grammar. My old English master hated the word 'nice' and told us not to use it because it doesn't mean anything. Well, Bill, I know you are no longer on earth, but I sometimes use 'nice' and it works nicely, thank you, so don't bother too much about such niceties and if appropriate there's nothing wrong with a bit of humour or slang. But there's lots wrong with jargon, so avoid it. A catchy headline grabs attention, so compose one and then if the first sentence is gripping and relevant there is a 50% chance they will read more. A lot might be skip-read apart from the last sentence and If that grips them the chances of them re-reading it all is increased. E-mail and sales-letter writing tricks can include a PS as these are sometimes looked at first, so the PS becomes a de facto headline.

Keep all letters and articles short (less = more) because people quickly lose interest. Assume that the reader has the attention span of a four year old, so make it clear, to the point and without waffle. It can be harder to write less than it is to write more and by attending a write-your-own-advertising seminar you can pick up writing skills.

Newsletters

With the possible exception of undertakers, most businesses can send tips to clients and prospects on how to improve their businesses, health, home or lifestyle. Try to include an offer, such as a discount (show the normal price to give the offer a value) and instead of the tiresome *for a limited time only* consider using something like, *this offer may be withdrawn without notice.*

Newsletters can be one page but if longer than two they risk not being read.Apart from an investment in time, it is not costly to produce newsletters and is free if emailed. Newsletters are though pointless if you don't have anyone to send them to and even if you do they may regard them as spam. A newsletter example is in the Appendices.

Other people's newsletters

Your tips might benefit customers of other businesses in which case you are contacting people you otherwise could not, so speak to businesses with similar customers to yours (who are not your rivals) to see if their customers, or suppliers, could benefit from what you can tell them – it needs to be hints and tips only and not hard selling. Newsletter writers find it hard to constantly find interesting fillers and if you have something interesting to their customers then you both benefit.

Press and magazine articles

Reasonable but not prize winning writing skills are needed for articles. Look at the writing style used in the publications you want to target and write your articles in the same style. Speak to the editor of the section you want your article to appear and ask if they would be interested. They may be if it contains new information and if so email the article and follow it up with a call. If they will not publish it ask them why. If it is because it's not relevant, choose another paper. If they say it's old-hat or self-advertising or lacking new information, thank them for their candour and rewrite it. The benefit of getting articles published is they give you credibility, which results in getting customers you otherwise might not get. Use your articles as publicity and show or email them to as many people as possible.

Summarise your free or low-cost options below:

Miser & Co advertising plan

What free advertising can I get?

From those I have helped   YES ☐ NO ☐ If YES, who ....

From other businesses   YES ☐ NO ☐ If YES, who ....

From my newsletters   YES ☐ NO ☐ If YES, who ....

From others newsletters   YES ☐ NO ☐ If YES, who ....

From articles   YES ☐ NO ☐ If YES, who ....

By networking   YES ☐ NO ☐ If YES, who ....

From referral alliances   YES ☐ NO ☐ If YES, who ....

What advertising will I have to pay for? ....

....

What will be the most effective media and why? ....

....

Paying for it

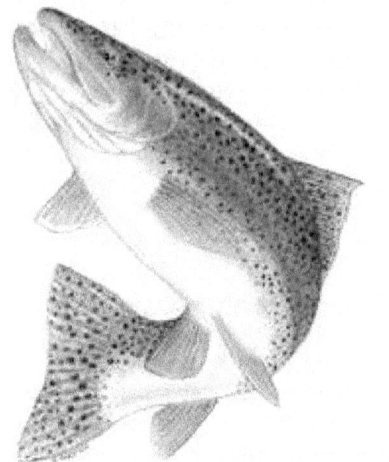

Learn the tricks of the advertising trade before shelling out cash by attending an advertising how-to seminar. You could possibly do so before quitting your job, so do a search to stop admen/girls netting you in costly fishy stuff like this:

A divisional manager said to me, "I'm firing the advertising agency."
"Why?" I asked,
"They want a fresh caught trout to photograph for a poster."
I said, "I suppose a stale old fish might look a bit dull."
He gave me a funny look and said, "They want a helicopter to collect it and fly it to their studio so it looks nice and fresh. It will cost $15,000."
I gave him a funny look, "You won't even get to eat it as we'll have to serve it to the chairman who might choke on it. Now, who's replacing them?"
He stopped looking at me funny, "They're in my office and would like to meet you."

The agency lost a $600,000pa account because of a fish, so be wary of hair-brained ideas, but unless *Miser & Co* can drum up business for free, some paid advertising may be needed. But keep your budget secret so it's not spent on trout. Spend as little as possible and make it as effective as possible. Give short shrift to o*ooh là là* media campaigns and where to photograph fish, so if zero and low-cost options are unusable (why?), options are:

Google Adwords pay-per-click

At time of writing, Google Adwords are the biggest pay-per-click advertising outfit but rivals are bound to challenge them. If you have a website look at *Adwords pay-per-click*. It's a sort-of auction and the highest bidder gets to the top of their search engine listings, so see if It could work for you. It is trial and error but once you get the hang of it, it's not that expensive.

Basic tips: Set a low daily budget until you get experience. Choose keywords to attract real customers and not tyre kickers. Keep the number of keywords to a minimum. Set a low click price and slowly increase it until you are on page 1. Unless you sell nationally use keywords applicable to your locality, such as *car valet (your suburb)*. Use the manual payment option - they don't like it because you control when and how much to top-up your account. Only run your ad when potential customers are likely to be searching (late at night is a waste of money for many businesses). By tweaking you can achieve a first page ranking at low cost provided you are selective and phrase specific with keywords.

You can learn a lot about it outside working hours. Start by experimenting with Google Adwords tutorials – they also give free one-to-one help on occasions so look out for their special offers.

It's hard to fool search engines but hordes of 'experts' claim they can get first page listings if you pay them - they can't all be right, can they? Google are not the only search engine, so look at their competitors to see what deals they have.

Social media

Social media, such as Facebook and the like, help sell stuff to *friends* and *friends of friends*. But unless you pay for category positioning you are unlikely to be near the top when someone keys in your equivalent of *teddy bears* because social media are businesses. Yet my wife gets sales for *teepees4kids* on Facebook at no cost, but not very many! Give it a go and see what happens and if it doesn't work consider paying for a trial campaign. It's fun learning the techniques out of working hours.

Advertising agencies

Advertising agencies charge for designing and placing adverts. They also receive discounts from TV, newspapers and other media which they may be disinclined to pass onto you. They invariably enquire about the size of your budget on the basis they need to know so they can plan your campaign – a side benefit is spending it all. As the owner of *Miser & Co* shy away from agencies unless you intend to spend a lot and need an agency to construct a campaign. Agencies can do spectacular campaigns that reap immense benefits for clients (they wouldn't last long otherwise) but for those starting a business on a limited budget, try DIY first.

There are niche agencies catering for smaller businesses and if you are an ad man or girl planning to start an agency that's how you might begin - and hopefully disprove my comments!

'The media'

In addition to competition 'the media' (TV, radio, newspapers, magazines, direct mail and so on) face from internet upstarts, there's a problem they try to bury and it's called '*repetition*'. So before deciding which media (they like being called that) to use look at **Ugly Features** further on.

Television

With local channels you don't need a big budget to appear on TV as some will compile a budget ad and throw in some airtime. If you look good on camera and your voice is right the channel might use you, then you'll be a TV star. But if you're not like that let them do it all *as the sole object is to sell!* If TV works for you (meaning your profit is far more than it costs) stick with it. The problem with TV adverts is the tendency of people to ignore them.

If you want to advertise on TV, watch other business's ads instead of ignoring them or fast forwarding. If you are selling locally, look at the ads of comparable businesses to yours and phone some to see if they make enough to justify the cost. They may tell you if you are not a competitor.

Radio

Listen to ads of businesses comparable to yours and phone some to see if they make enough to justify the cost. To get a feel, listen to ads on stations your potential customers might tune into, but if your competitors don't advertise on them they either haven't thought of it, or more likely, have tried it and it didn't work – in which case, why would it work for you?

Listen to radio adverts before contacting radio reps, or them contacting you, to reduce the risk of being seduced by their propaganda. A thing to remember about radio is that (at time of writing) there is no such thing as *visual radio* so adverts lack pictures. That means ads have to be more punchy than those on TV or print to stimulate listeners to buy and a jingle may help unless you are a funeral director. If your name is Sam and you sell used cars, maybe "Slippery Sam the used car man; phone 1800 bangers," could be a jingle (well, perhaps not quite that) but ask the reps which ads work, which don't and why.

Print advertising

© and courtesy of
www.freekingnews.com

Newspapers, magazines, direct mail, posters, brochures and everything else that is printed still make up the biggest advertising sector (at time of writing).

Print is a hard sector because each advert competes with those of non-competitors for the readers' time. Toothpaste compete with holidays, cars and everything else because no matter what print medium you use, others use it too. That means your ad must be strikingly different to others, such as Crust toothpaste.

Newspapers

Circulation claims such as *delivered to 25,000 homes* doesn't mean they are actually read. Statistics from a major Sunday paper showed that each one was read by sixteen people - they must queue up or have extra-large families. Regional/national papers suffer from circulation decline, but are more likely to be read than freebies because people tend to read stuff they buy. Another positive paid-for papers have is there are now fewer adverts than in the past. Whilst that is not positive for them it is for advertisers because there is less competition for readers' attention.

If you advertise in papers do so in those with readers who are likely to buy your products (remember Oracle's products beat services example). Next, check your ads positioning as it is a waste of money to advertise women's fashions next to a handyman article because most of your target market will not see it.

Magazines

It usually costs more to advertise in magazines than in newspapers but they have longer shelf lives and offer a better chance of reaching the right audience. Advertising stuff in Women's Weekly may work for women's power tools but not for men's, so identify those appropriate to your business.

Carefully select your media to avoid aiming your equivalent of a lawn mower ad at apartment dwellers. Unless you are doing a one-off advert for-a-limited-time-only special, an issue with print ads is repetition as shown in the **Ugly Features chart** over the page.

Ugly features

The ugly feature of TV, radio, newspaper, magazine and other print advertising are people ignoring your advert. This means it has to be repeated before it is noticed, which is an ugly feature media reps are shy of revealing.

Ugly Features - Retention by Repetition	
TIMES INSERTED	**AWARENESS**
1st	2% - 5%
2nd	6% - 10%
3rd	11% - 17%
4th	18% - 30%
5th	31% - 44%
6th	+ 70%
Source: *Direct Marketing Association*	

To overcome the repetition problem, newspapers and magazines give discounts for repeat insertions which, from their point of view, is good for business because you spend more money. Apart from limited-time impulse offers where one or two insertions might work, the *Ugly Features* chart shows how many times an advert has to appear before it is noticed. If you are advertising in a medium your target market is likely to read (why waste money advertising in media they will not read?) then after 6 or so insertions around 70% will have seen your ad. A proportion of the market will have seen it every insertion (2% to 5%) whilst 17% should have seen it three times. Your message might then begin to stick but it's costly. Attending a suitable advertising seminar can soon pay for itself.

Write your own adverts

DIY is fun and gets even better if you are short of money, so before paying someone see if you can write your own adverts by attending that advertising seminar I mentioned. You'll learn what can work and what won't, so put the cost of the seminar into your advertising budget. You will meet people from different industries so why not suggest starting a network? Also, look at adverts of competitors and those with customers similar to yours to get free ideas on writing your own ads – junk mail can do the same, so read some of it!

Faxes

Faxes are not used much anymore and even when they were high-tech, success rates for fax-outs varied from poor to abysmal.

Telemarketing

Telemarketing gets a mention in case you thought I had overlooked it - for many businesses it should be overlooked. But if you love unsolicited phone calls during dinner, telemarketing might be for you although if the person is on a *Do Not Call Register* you face stiff fines if you call. If you also love being told to go away, do the telemarketing yourself, but if not consider appointing a telemarketer. If you want to know more see **Telemarketing** in the Appendices.

Sponsorships

Sponsorship can be costly and unless it brings in enough business to justify the cost it is really a donation. Sponsorships by big companies are often done for public relations reasons and not as advertising needs. One of the companies I was CEO of sponsored motorcycle racing, coastguard and marine events, including ocean yacht racing - the latter paid for by our overseas parent as no way Mr. Miser would spend *that* amount of money.

Travel

The author's little trip around Australia

There's nothing like a bit of travel to empty the pockets. I became a travel connoisseur which was most enjoyable, especially side shows put on by our suppliers - ballooning in France and sailing in Japan – but the author did pay for this year long trip with his wife around Australia.

A lot of business travel is unnecessary and taxmen think so too as they look closely at it, especially if it was incurred before you actually started the business - they usually disallow it.

If you are starting a window cleaning, plumbing or other local business or practice you probably don't need to travel unless it's for up-skilling or similar reasons. But if you make things or wholesale them and want to sell nationally or internationally travel is needed. But avoid wandering too far because potential customers are only suspect customers despite what they say. This is especially true in USA and the intoxicating words "it's a done deal" can be enough to get you on the next plane. Hesitate before going because the term *done deal* can mean you are being done and if they are that interested send samples, or get them to visit you by offering a discount on the first order if they sign-up. That can be cheaper than you visiting them.

Only travel when you are sure it will pay for itself. To reduce temptation, get emotional and think about coming home dejected. To keep the emotions churning, think about plane crashes. Unless things have recently changed, what happens when a wide-bodied plane ditches is that the captain drops one wing into the water, which causes the plane to slew. When the engine hits the water the impact rips the wing off and if that doesn't split the fuselage into bits it sure does when the other wing hits. It then fills with water and sinks and that's when the sea is calm. When rough it's quicker. Next comes terrorism and it pays to have at least two passports: one from a hefty country and the other from a rich non-offensive neutral. Use on the spot judgement to decide which one to ditch. Have a nice trip.

Exhibitions

Modest-size local exhibitions can be low cost (if pricy think twice) and effective. But those who make money from big exhibitions are the organizers. If you are selling *I'll buy it right now products*, then rent a cheap stall in a corner at big exhibitions – the type that costs a fortune to attend for exhibitors with large stands.

Unless they are trade shows, tyre-kickers are a problem and exhibitions are where they kick them. Some exhibitors are happy with the outcome and are the ones quoted in promoters' propaganda. So before spending anything, dress smartly, take your business cards and go to a suitable exhibition shortly before closing time on the final day to study exhibitor expressions. Ask some if it has been worthwhile and would they exhibit again. Some will have leads, others will have made sales and a number will shake their heads. If it is an up-market exhibition the organizers often throw an exhibitor cocktail-do at the end, so tell them you are a potential exhibitor and want to stay for a few minutes to gauge exhibitor feelings. Because you look smart and have a business card they might agree, but if they fob you off and exhibitors look glum, well …

Junk mail and other advertising

There's lots of junk mail and according to the Direct Marketing Association it's increasing. *The Economist* states that in 2013 $170 billion was spent on physical and electronic junk mail in America. *The Economist* found some interesting statistics which state that junk mail "conversion rates" (meaning sales from sending the stuff) are 3% for unsolicited adverts sent through the post, 0.1% for electronic ads (spam) and a minutely-whopping 0.01% for online adverts. Perhaps now's the time to go to a DIY advertising seminar?

Other forms of paid-for adverts include Yellow Pages which are now mainly online, but do you want 0.01% success? If Adwords and other low/non-cost ads can bring in enough business you won't need to shell-out cash on directories. No doubt other forms of advertising will emerge as time goes on, but whether they will work any better than the current stuff depends – I'm sure the promoters' statistics will be glowing.

Tally-ho and off you go

Use the *Advertising Slasher* at the chapter's end to see how little you really need to spend and how to spend it. Without rubbing it in, if you start a business you avoid inheriting the previous owner's advertising budget - you just might be tempted to follow it without exploring other options.

Charge of the Light Brigade (1854) Crimean War. 670 set out
and official casualties were 278. Painted by William Simpson

The charge of the Light Brigade increased the British
Army's prestige – their leaders lost theirs. Plan your campaign
well to waste as little money as possible. You'll be lucky to spend
every cent well but sound planning can limit losses to a few
dollars instead of big bucks, so use the 'Slasher' on the next
page.

Start your tally-ho and put free-of-charge first ...

Miser & Co Advertising Slasher

When will I attend an advertising seminar? If not , why not ....

....……………………………………...

Suitable seminar presenters are: ....

…………………………………………………………………………………...

Who will design/print my business card? ....

What free advertising can I get ....

....

Do I need an advertising agent? If YES, why and who ....…...

…………………………………………………………………………………...

.

What else do I need and how much will it cost (approx) ....…...

…………………………………………………………………………………...

…………………………………………………………………………………...

…………………………………………………………………………………...

9____ Reasons for *not* buying a business or a franchise

Some advisers like crowing that 70% of start-ups fail, which is why they claim its safer to buy a business than starting one.

Be careful a seller doesn't
gurgle your money
(photo: under the author's kitchen sink)

The 70% failure figure is a myth because it comes from an assumption. The assumption is that the reason why businesses (new and old) vanish is because they go broke. But there are other causes, such as theft by Martians, mergers, buyers who buy the assets only and not the company which owns them for reasons shown later. So, barring bad luck and provided you plan it well, your soon-to-be business can be as safe – if not safer - than buying one.

Of course some new businesses fail. So do established ones - and franchises. No one really knows what the true failure rate of new start-ups is, but it's unlikely to be 70%, or anything close to it. Also, nobody knows what the true failure rate is of those who buy an existing business. So if somebody claims that the failure rate of established businesses is much lower than for new businesses, ask where they got the figures from – are they assumptions or are they accurate statistics? Remember what 19th century British Prime Minister Benjamin Disraeli's said; "There are three kinds of lies: lies, damned lies, and statistics."

But if you are going into business explore every option, including buying one or buying a franchise.

Buying a business (franchises are next)

The first question to ask is, *why is it for sale*? You are unlikely to be told it's going broke even if that's the real reason. They are more likely to say the vendor has health problems, wants to *move-on*, or retire or something. Health, moving-on and the something's need looking into. Retiring is plausible if the vendor is old and also if the vendor is younger and made a fortune from the business - the accounts will show if it's currently true (but it doesn't mean it will continue to boom). Moving on, or something, can mean the business is about to slip into the mire, products are poor or almost obsolete or the sector is about to undergo a, err, *paradigm shift* - that means it's dying on its feet, or the changes are so big it will cost heaps to tackle them, so find out.

To avoid wasting money, do the initial finding-out yourself. If the vendor has a medical problem make sure it's genuine – an unhealthy pallor is an indication. If the business is running-down the state of the equipment, inventory, premises and the accounts are indicators, so ask to see them without signing anything apart from (perhaps) a confidentiality agreement but read it carefully beforehand and if uneasy don't sign it without striking out undesirable clauses – don't be shy, just do it! Buying the assets of a run-down business cheaply could enable you to build it up, provided you are certain it can be done and there is no risk of killing your creativity or depriving you of the money to develop new opportunities.

If you want to buy the assets only buy those you need. They may insist you buy the lot and only you can decide whether to do so. But avoid buying intangibles - debtors, creditors and staff commitments, such as holiday (vacation) entitlements, pension and redundancy costs. It is easy to get ensnared by these and other traps, so be careful.

If you want to go further, be prepared to pay an experienced accountant to verify everything. Do they really own the assets' or are they secured by a bank, financier or anybody else under the Personal Property Securities Act or other laws? Unless this is thoroughly checked they could be seized and sold under your feet and you won't get a cent. **So, is buying a business really safer than starting one?**

If you're still keen after all this, a detailed due diligence should reveal how things are, but may not unearth what the vendor is hiding. Unless you are an accountant or lawyer this is the time you may need one or both. But before going to that expense have a chat first.

Fireside chat

There's nothing like a fireside chat to discover what a business is like. It saves heaps on professional fees, so if you are interested in buying it visit the vendor's home. If it's a partnership or a company with several shareholders, visit as many as feasible – start with the one who brags most.

If you don't get an invitation, engineer one: "Where did you say you live? That's good as I need to see my cousin on Saturday who lives close by, so can I pop in?" Where and how they live says a lot about their business. A 'nice' home doesn't have to be flashy because what matters is: *Does it reflect what they tell you about their business?* An extravagant home might be heavily in hock, whilst a well tended one that matches what they told you about their business is more likely to mean they are truthful, organized and have pride in what they own. Old cars on a lawn with grass so high it would hide an elephant, fast food cartons strewn around and mouldy dishes in the kitchen doesn't necessarily mean their business is in a similar mess. But it's a pretty good bet it is.

Personnel recruiters – oops, human resource (HR) specialists - and savvy employers like home visits. Whilst they might not go into a short-listed candidate's home they often drive by it. Do likewise if you can't get an invite. Then phone the vendor at around nine one evening to see if they are on the 'turps. If they are it's a little warning. Do the same when you employ people, but try not to be on the 'turps yourself at the time!

Paddy's paddock

If their home isn't up to much and there's no boat apart from an old tinny in a shed, it might just be possible they are kidding about their little gold mine, so get turnover and expense warranties at the least. If they say sales are $290,000 a year for a thirty-hour week and expanses are only $12,000, get them to put it in writing. Ask for proof. Where's the money gone? It certainly hasn't gone into their home.

"Oh, you go on round-the-world holidays because you only need to work six months a year and have a Swiss bank account! Wow, that's nice. Can I see the photos, passport and a peep at that Union Bank of Switzerland passbook please? I know it's a bit personal, but if I'm going to buy your little gold mine, surely you won't mind proving there is more to it than that old ladder and rusty truck out back."

Whether you run like mad right now depends entirely on their reaction. If they only show you photos of a tent in Paddy's Paddock, or photos of a seedy resort, thank them kindly and walk briskly away.

If you have found a sound business (or franchise) to buy at a sensible price, then to help reduce accountancy/legal fees see **Buying a Business** in the Appendices.

Buying a franchise

Hesitate before buying a franchise if you are an entrepreneur because you will ultimately – possibly quickly - become unhappy for reasons explained in the *Get going* chapter.

There are other reasons, such as the little matter that *you never truly own your business!*

This is an extract of what Prof Lorelle Frazer co author of a This is a summary of what Prof Lorelle Frazer co author of a report on Australian franchising said to News.com.au "Franchisees still enter franchising without doing their homework

- 49 per cent said they went into a particular franchise based on their gut feeling. Many do not understand what is involved. We interviewed one man and he said he had no idea that it would involve getting up at 2am - but he had bought a bakery franchise. What did he expect was going to happen?"

The benefits of buying an established and well-known franchise are the business systems, brands and other attributes. But some benefits are for people who want to move into an industry in which they have little experience, such as a former banker buying a bakery franchise (I know one who almost did but it was 2am starts that put him off). Lack of industry experience was discussed earlier and is a major risk because prospective franchisees might not have the knowledge to calculate what the threats to the sector are.

Before buying a franchise do the same checks as you would if buying any other business. In particular, speak to their franchisees to see how happy and successful they are. To protect them from being pestered by tyre-kickers, franchisors often only permit this when they are pretty sure you are genuinely interested. Fair enough because if you were a franchisee you probably wouldn't like to be pestered. But if they try to deter you from speaking to any franchisees be a bit suspicious because to paraphrase William Shakespeare, *things may not be well in the franchise of Denmark.* Don't buy until you speak to several franchisees of YOUR choice and get the franchisor to give you a full list of franchisees so you can choose in case they steer you to pet ones. It's likely that not all franchisees will be totally happy and it's revealing to speak to some unhappy ones because you can discover if the reasons are gripes or real problems.

Franchising propaganda claims that the failure rate for franchisees is around 6%. But where does the 6% come from? From statistics of course, but they could more flawed than the 70% failure rate for new businesses. What makes them less reliable is they come from members of franchise associations. It might just be possible there are errors or omissions as it is hard for associations to do audits and possibly little incentive to do them.

Another franchise feature is you never own the business you think you have bought. Not only do you pay what can be a whopping sum for the franchise fee, you ultimately lose it because what is euphemistically called 'an investment' is actually rent. The reality is that a franchise is a lease and at some point it expires and the up-front rent you paid is not refundable. You also pay royalties, advertising levies and possibly a mark-up on goods or services provided by the franchisor. Once-upon-a-time some franchise agreements were in perpetuity but this is rare now, yet most franchise agreements have renewal clauses to cushion the termination feature, but almost invariably a renewal fee and legal costs are payable. To avoid termination, franchisees can sell their franchise to a new entrant (you perhaps?) so ensure you can do the same before you buy. There are likely to be transfer fees and legal costs, so negotiate on who pays them or a percentage split because you may be asked the same when it's your turn to sell.

There are termination clauses in agreements which are in the franchisor's favour. If you breach them the franchisor can terminate you. They can do it quickly if you are in arrears with royalty or other payments. Termination can be for reasons such as bringing the franchise into disrepute (that can mean almost anything) so the agreement needs carful vetting by a specialist – the bill will be yours. Also, restraint of trade clauses may be in it, so on termination not only do you lose your business, you can be prevented from engaging in a similar one in future.

Such fascinating features are not prominently displayed in the propaganda. Yes, you will, err, should, make a profit but it's not guaranteed - if it is there can be so many fish hooks it's a wonder there are any fish left. Then there is the risk that the franchise system is defective, goes out of fashion or the franchisor goes broke.

If you are keen to buy a franchise see a specialist franchise lawyer or accountant before signing anything. Their fees could be more than those incurred in starting a business, so unless you are dead sure that buying a franchise (or other business) is in your best interest, why not use the money to start your own show?

10___Raising the cash

Make your friendly personal bank your
lender of last choice.

Most people wanting to borrow money for a business make their personal bank the first port of call. Be different and make it your last then if things go bad you might only lose your business and not your home.

Before looking at money lenders look at the alternatives, such as *crowdfunding* but if you have to go to a moneylender put your personal bank at the bottom of the pile.

During the American War of Independence John Adams, a future president, went to Holland which was then Europe's centre of borrowing to raise cash for the war. Mr Adams said seeking loans in Amsterdam "resembled that of a man in the midst of the ocean negotiating for his life among a school of sharks." You may find the same attitude if you borrow money and have problems paying it back (or paying the interest) so put banks at the end of the list, especially the one your home loan is with.

Money may have to come from your own pocket, but make it is as little as possible because there are better funding options – and your own pocket includes pledging your home as security. If after reading this chapter you still need to borrow money from potential shark-like sources (no matter how nice they were when you arranged the loan) arrange protection on your assets, especially your home.

Before scraping-up money find ways to save it by only buying stuff when it's needed and not because it makes you feel good. When, or if, you need to buy try and obtain credit as shown in the *Cunning plan* chapter. If buying it will drain you, lease it or outsource the tasks because then you won't need to buy it. If buying stuff will lower costs and improve efficiency or quality then do so when you can afford it.

Another money-saver is not having premises. Blue Nile, who claims to be the leading online diamond and jewellery retailer, has no shops (see *www.bluenile.com*). If they can do it, can you? A bit of imagination and investigation could get you underway until you can afford premises. By that stage you might not need any.

Crowdfunding, venture capital, business angels and Aunt Maud

New ways of raising money have emerged, such as *crowdfunding* – do an online search. Crowdfunding is a form of venture capital provided by groups of people (*the crowd*) who pool money or other resources for ventures. There are two main types of crowdfunding; equity-based and donation-based – the latter is where investments or donations of some sort are made in exchange for a return later on – it can even be a non-monetary, such as goods or services. If you have something that attracts crowdfunders you could be in business without borrowing much.

Unless you are starting what is likely to become a very big business the large venture capital outfits may not be interested, but as things can change rapidly it's worth looking into. But don't spend much time on it because they even turned down Skype (founded by two Scandinavians in 2003) because it was too small.

Next, look at *business angels* - the difference between venture capital providers and business angels is that angels look at smaller businesses and new start-ups. Whilst they are similar to crowdfunders they include lawyers and accountants who manage clients' funds, individuals, investor groups plus friends and relatives. Lawyers and accountants are a cautious bunch (they have to be to avoid being struck-off) so they are likely to demand securities similar to what the banks want, but they are still worth contacting – it's also a free way of getting your business plan checked! Write to them (yes, write a personal letter and mail it instead of emailing as they will at least read a letter) then phone to see if they are interested. Whilst it's OK to make private approaches, it is illegal to invite the public to invest in your business without having a formal prospectus and complying with strict rules, so be careful with the wording and say it is a private approach and not an invitation to the public to invest. If you decide to advertise, do the same.

Also, make a list of people who could invest in your venture, including friends and relatives such as Aunt Maud, because if your business is sound they can make money too. Whether their investment should be interest bearing loans or shares is for negotiation, but the real profits (and risks) come from shareholdings. Whilst you would be diluting yours by inviting others to invest, it avoids paying interest and repaying the money. If they are lending money they may want securities, but if things go wrong you could possibly negotiate a better withdrawal with friends and family than banks would agree to. But do not hoodwink them into making an unwise investment by glossing over risks, or lying.

Other shareholders

If you intend to go into business with others they must be willing to invest their money otherwise why go into business with them? Will they be hands-on and work with you full or part time or will they be passive investors like Aunt Maud? If you find the right people it could help your business expand quicker and solve some (or all) of the funding problem. List those with the money and expertise and personalities who could be interested. If no one comes to mind work out how to find them - you may know colleagues who could be interested, such as those who are disgruntled withy their job, about to retire or are retired but bored and would like to keep their hand-in by parking some money into your enterprise and helping it grow.

Equipment leasing

If you really do need equipment which you can't afford to buy then lease it like my dentist friend did. But if you are a dentist, or other professional, be careful not to over commit yourself by buying expensive stuff which you could do without for the time being. An advantage of leasing is the only security most lease companies usually want is title to the assets being leased, but you still have to pay the lease charges. So, do you really need the stuff?

Vendor finance

Buying a business or a franchise can sometimes have the advantage of vendor finance.

Instead of being cheeky and asking for payment by instalments right at the start, break the assets into bits. If you are buying machinery or equipment ask them for a gesture of its reliability by saying something like; "I'm sure you have lovingly maintained it like your garden lawn (the one with the food cartons and elephant grass) so it won't break down will it? Great, then you won't mind putting your personal money where your business mouth is and accepting 33% on hand-over with the rest payable in ... months or ......years."

If bits of equipment can be sold at a profit after you take over, sell them, but if the vendor retains title (which they should until you have paid in full) you may have to pay them out when you sell it. Next look at the inventory and instead of refusing to buy the obsolete bits, offer to buy some of it at a reduced price and on credit: "I'll take that pile of ... at 50% off and pay you if and when I sell it. As I'm taking a risk, how about me paying for the rest in instalments too?' If they agree you can sell it and pay after you get paid.

Do the same with fittings, office equipment, vehicles and everything else you can think of. To avoid being too cheeky, pay cash for the petty cash tin and contents. But only pay cash for things you can cuddle or tap with a hammer and that excludes debtors and goodwill - never ever take responsibility for paying creditors or loans etc. If you are buying the debtors, only pay for them when the debtors pay you and not beforehand. Then try and get an extra month's credit by saying that because you will be working as their unpaid credit controller, it would be fair to hand over the money at the end of the following month. If you pay goodwill, then because it cannot be hugged or tapped, pay for it out of the profits after they are earned.

Finally, never tell a vendor, or anybody else for that matter, especially banks, how much cash or assets you have. Vendors can be sympathetic to giving credit if they have confidence in you and feel (feelings can be important) the only thing blocking the deal is a minor cash issue. If they think you can pay more up-front they may try and get you to do so.

Franchisor finance

If you are buying a newly established franchise and are one of their pioneers, get the franchisor to share the risks to prove they are confident in their systems. Professional service franchises can be the easiest to persuade because providing the finance does not involve them shelling out their own cash. So if you are buying a professional service franchise – or any other franchise for that matter - ask for terms.

Expect to pay up-front for premises, fit out and equipment, but ask for terms on their systems and intellectual property. They might accept 50% (try for less) with the balance payable over time, so ask. They can only say no and you can also walk away. If they say yes refuse to give security on your home or other assets.

When buying a franchise from an outgoing franchisee, have your cake and eat it by asking for terms from the franchisee and franchisor! Ask the outgoing franchisee for terms then be a bit cheeky and ask the franchisor for a royalty holiday or extended credit for the first six months on supplies they provide. Say you know they charge transfer fees because you've read their franchise agreement. Mention that your advisor suggests that as they are getting a chunk of money for doing nothing, apart from giving you a bit of training, it's reasonable to extend credit on their windfall. They might agree to some of it.

Property leases.

Try to get better terms from the landlord by pointing out the horrible cracks, lack of parking, cramped yard, lack of foot traffic and hint that you might not want to operate the business from their premises, but might if they give you a rent holiday (say three months rent free) or did some alterations. Depending on the state of the market they may agree.

Other borrowing possibilities

You may think the author needs his head read with some of some of the following. They are included because they have worked and you will never know which may work for you unless you give some or all a go!

Borrow from the vendor's bank.

This is not as cheeky as it seems. If you are buying a business and can't find any other finance other than a bank, then consider approaching the vendor's bank - hopefully it's not a branch of your bank. The vendor's expression when you ask him to come along for the introduction can tell you far more than you have learned so far! Stammering might mean their little gold mine is not that golden and the bank is about to foreclose. If that's the case it could be worthwhile visiting their bank but if the vendor comes along you don't want them hanging around for long, so boot them out after five minutes. If the bank is about to foreclose and you are a possible saviour, fight tooth and nail to avoid giving security on your home and because they are not your bank they might agree if they get some other security. If you have it only disclose enough to get them interested and not the lot as they will want the lot if you do. If they insist on more, disclose a bit more but not the lot unless you really must and do your best to avoid it even if means killing the deal. Finally, avoid getting your spouse to sign a personal guarantee.

 If the bank says no, or only agrees to partial finance, the vendor might agree to terms to save the deal. At this point business brokers become great allies - they smell their commission and twisting the vendor's arm is the way to get it.

Borrowing from other banks and your bank

Approach other banks first and make appointments with their Business Managers (some call them Commercial Managers). Patience is needed as the objective is to find a bright spark instead of a damp squib. Say: "I'm looking for a banker who wants to be a mover and shaker. If you are that person tell me what you can really do?" One might say "That's me, so sit down and tell me what you want and I will tell you what I can do."

Such meetings can have more value than just than wanting to borrow money. Ask what other sources of finance they know of, such as that from wealthy customers. Some may be interested in venture finance and their expertise could help your business. Even if nothing comes of your search for a cavalier banker, you will gain experience of what other banks want for lending you money. Odds are it will be similar to your bank – security on your home - but now you will know the negotiation tactics to use if you approach your bank. Start by saying that the security you will give should only be a 'floating charge" (or similar) on your business's assets. Only concede more if forced to and suggest a debenture mortgage (now hard to get, but try) is the most you can give.

Get the credit

If you will be buying stuff regularly, ask the supplier for credit and then buy at the beginning of each month. That way you get two months interest free credit on a 30 day account. But dress smart as nobody in their right mind gives credit to scruffs - there's nothing wrong with overalls, but let Len launder them first. If they want your ongoing business they should grant credit, so tell them that giving you credit is a condition of purchase if there are other suppliers to choose from. When you get credit, pay on due date to establish a good credit record for future referral purposes.

Read their Terms and Conditions of Trade *before signing them* and try to avoid a personal guarantee, which some ask for. Smart businesses sometimes disguise a guarantee as a solvency declaration clause to make you liable if your business defaults and it may be hard to reject it – if you sell on credit you too should have one.

Write it down. In the margins write down which of the above could work for you, who to approach and when.

11_____Up and running

The mulch machine is up-and-running

You've raised the cash, got a good deal on equipment, have potential customers lined up and everything's in place to churn out the first batch of garden mulch. Great, but what about the odds-and-ends of running it?

Business-folk are often less than thrilled with stuff like accounts and admin, but getting to grips with some of it can save you lots of money, and that's great fun.

Time

They don't make time anymore, so use it or lose it. List what your *real priorities* are because time is what you are selling and it's nice to know how much you earn to see if it's more than it would be if you worked for somebody else. Keeping a timesheet shows how long you work and how well you use your time and dividing the profit by hours worked shows what your hourly earnings are. If it's less than what you got as an employee (or less than what your own employees get which can happen) something's wrong.

When starting a business it can take time to get your earnings cranked up, so keep the timesheet going until it is and repeat the exercise every six months or so to see if you are still using time well. A simple one is over the page.

Miser & Co.

Time Sheet

Date	Start time	Finish time	Time spent	How the time was spent

A time sheet shows how you spend time and using time well is the cheapest resource to fix. Eliminate whatever stops you from making a decent income otherwise your business will under-perform and the longer it does the greater the risk of failure.

Use this to work out your priorities:-

My time priorities are

Earning a good living? YES ❐ NO ❐ Reasons ....

....

Growing my business? YES ❐ NO ❐ Reasons ....

....

Cashflow management? YES ❐ NO ❐ Reasons ....

....

Am I achieving all the above? YES ❐ NO ❐ Reasons ....

....

If not, am using my time well? YES ❐ NO ❐ Reasons ....

....

I can overcome them by:- ....
Cont'd next page

....

Engaging somebody YES ❐ NO ❐ Reasons ....

....

If YES – full time YES ❐ NO ❐ Reasons ....

....

part time YES ❐ NO ❐ Reasons ....

....

Casual/contract YES ❐ NO ❐ Reasons ....

....

Will outsourcing improve my/my staff's productivity YES ❐ NO ❐ Reasons

....

If YES, what can I outsource? ....

....

Can I manage my staff better YES ❐ NO ❐ Reasons ....

....

Do I need to contact/see customers for repeat or new business? YES ❐ NO ❐

Reasons...

....

Do I need to improve factory or shop efficiency? YES ❐ NO ❐ Reasons ......

....

If YES , how? ....

....

Hiring and firing

Hiring

If you work much more than 40 hours a week you'll soon be a very dull boy or girl, so be daring and hire somebody if your business is doing well. If you can't afford or justify full time staff, hire them on a casual, contract or outsource basis.

As mentioned near the beginning of this book be a funny ha-ha boss and not a funny-peculiar one. A few laughs and a joke can make their day (and yours) enjoyable. Show them the priorities, keep them informed, give compliments and if ticking them off do it discretely, but it's wise to have a witness just in case. Sticking to this helps avoid most employment problems.

If you need casual or part timers, ask around or place a job ad on a supermarket noticeboard (often free) before advertising. Using HR firms is costly but saves screening candidates as you only interview short listed ones. It also reduces the risk of hiring wrong-bods, so if using a HR outfit, check they offer guarantees for faulty candidate selection. They may also provide you with an employment agreement - it may even be free.

"1999 to 2004 are blank because I was drummer on the *Dead and Alive* world tour."

Check job gaps in case they were in jail or drying out – the following is a true story from my friend who was CEO of an African building firm (a subsidiary of a big Irish outfit) who temporarily needed a long-span roofing expert. Their Dublin head office sent one out after only doing a cursory reference check and he was late for work the first day (jetlag you know), even later the next (still recovering from it) and didn't pitch up at all on the third. The hotel then sent a bill for damages as he had set his room alight with a cigarette when blind drunk.

Firing

Unless you find it fun, firing people isn't nice. If you have to fire someone doing so properly can save you from grievance and other claims.

Treat staff as you would like to be treated and give them a fair trial before the hanging. Seriously though, give them the opportunity of fixing things to reduce the risk of a wrongful dismissal claim. Keep calm and never fire anybody out of hand. Do any disciplining discretely and away from customers or other staff, but have at least one reliable witness present. Follow the session up with a written warning and keep a copy as evidence if they lodge a claim against you. Whilst such things change and depending what state or country you are in, two or three warnings before a firing is usually acceptable. Instant dismissal can be OK if the offence is severe, but ensure it is well documented and you have reliable witnesses.

Before employing staff, have an employment agreement in place - if using a HR outfit they might give/sell you one, but if not get one from a lawyer which is cheaper than having your socks sued-off later. If you have time, consider going to a short seminar to keep pace with employment obligations.

Safety

The days of pit ponies and child labour are gone, so make your workplace safe. Pop-in out of working hours and ask yourself: "Would I feel safe working here?" Take a friend along and ask him/her too.

If equipment, goggles and fire extinguishers etc actually work and legs are firmly fixed to chairs you are sort-of OK. Whilst about it, check that the floor is not slippery, carpets can't be tripped over, the kettle cord is not naked and the nuclear reactor's cracked casing has been glued. Keep up-to-date with regulations and using common sense can save you from being sued - bring in an expert if in doubt, but preferably not the one who set his hotel room alight.

Accounts

Accounts are great fun if you are making a profit. Besides, it's nice to know how you're doing and those who have loaned you money might be interested too.

If you don't know where you are, you won't know where you are going and finding out is more fun than just doing the boring old books. They're not boring at all if someone else does them free of charge, such as your spouse, and a bookkeeper won't charge much if you give them easy-to-follow records. Internet banking is easy, so is maintaining running totals of your bank balance on chequebook stubs - don't laugh they still have their uses – you can stop payment on a cheque but can't on internet banking.

If you have lots of money that's real fun but whilst keeping an eye on the cash is OK for day-to-day running a bit more is needed for steering your ship. Accounts are your ship's chart to keep it off the rocks – there won't be rocks if you are making a tidy profit and have kept aside enough money to pay creditors and taxes.

If doing the accounts yourself interrupts you from making a living, outsource it.

Getting customers to pay

There's no problem getting customers to pay if yours is a cash-only business, which includes EFT and credit cards that pay their merchants promptly - some card companies don't pay promptly and charge high commissions, so be like other businesses and don't accept them. But if you have to sell on credit make sure you get paid on time and chase slow payers by reading the *Credit Control chapter.* A droopy bank balance can indicate that customers are not paying so check it often - other reasons for being short of cash come later.

Checking your money level is more important than checking your car's fuel level. Getting a lift for fuel is embarrassing, but running out of cash is catastrophic if the bank refuses to top-you-up. They may at some stage, so it's very dangerous to skip checking your bank balance because you could go out of business. If you can't check it (why can't you?) get your spouse or bookkeeper to do it then find who is not paying and why and use the Credit Control chapter to fix it.

Paying the bills

Paying creditors on time gives you a good credit record to get more credit from others, so try to pay on time. If lack of time is the problem, get your spouse or bookkeeper to pay your creditors – but make sure you trust them as you will be giving them access to your bank account, so ask your bank about controls, such as maximum withdrawal limits.

If occasionally you can't pay on time because you are short of money, don't fret because it happens to the best of businesses. Find out why you are short of cash – are customers not paying on time, have you got too much inventory or are sales down? The **Credit Control and Bogeymen** chapters may help you fix them.

Customers

Customer hunting is fun and when you have got them buy key ones lunch now and again. Be bold and find out what they think of you - and your competitors, and why to get ideas on how to get more business, new customers or to fix problems to keep them as customers. Free lunches can be good for business.

Customers are not kings, they are emperors with power of life and death over your business. No matter what your business is, you will be out of business if they stop using you. If you sell one-off products, such as life or medical insurance or are a divorce lawyer, you kill your customers after the first sale because they don't normally need you again, or at least not for a long time, so you have to find new ones. That could mean you have to spend more on advertising than those with repeat customers.

If you have repeat customers try to get them to buy from you more often. Depending on what you do, loyalty programs, such as discounts after a certain number of purchases or dollars spent, can bring customers back sooner. Whilst loyalty programs are a bit overdone they can work, which is why they are used.

Write down what you can do below. Also, keep the law firm that offered credit management seminars in mind because it might stimulate you to find new opportunities that your competitors have not thought of.

This is how I can get more business

Inventories/stocks

Unless you are a service provider you are bound to have stocks of some kind. Stocks drain cashflows, so keep them low and if you have 30th of the following month payment terms with your suppliers remember to order at the beginning of the month to get sixty days credit. To combat this, canny suppliers have special offers expiring on the last day of the month and if your customers buy-up big at the beginning of each month, do the same.

When I was CEO of the company that disliked trout we had a big dealer who bought all his stocks at the beginning of the month. If he needed more during the month he asked for immediate delivery but for it to be invoiced the beginning of the next month (his brother, an accountant, taught him this). If we were overstocked our general manager sometimes agreed, but when he refused the dealer phoned me for a reversal. To overcome this the general manager and I agreed on what to say in advance and it worked as long as he got his way, or part of it, occasionally.

Cost creep

Costs have a nasty creeping habit, so regularly put on your miser hat to see by looking at your zero-based budget then say the magic words: *"Creepy cost cutter's here again."*

Costs, such as travel, are creep prone. You might have culled the temptation to participate in exhibitions, but finding out what's new by visiting a trade show in Las Vegas might replace it. If going is likely to make you more money than it costs then go, but be honest with yourself and if it's only a maybe then ask the organizers who the exhibitors are and visit their websites instead. Below are examples of costs that commonly creep:

Miser & Co Creeping Cost Cutter			
Expenses	Budget	Actual	Reasons for difference
Travel	$		
Power/fuel	$		
Entertainment	$		
Raw materials	$		
Bought in goods/stocks	$		
Other creeping costs I may have to watch-out for are:			
....	$		
....	$		
....	$		

Riots and things

"Are we covered for riots?" my insurance friend's South American client asked on the phone. My pal said, *"No, and why do you ask?"*

"There's a riot outside and we need it right now," came the reply. My friend said, *"We can insure you for the next riot but not this one."* What mean friends I have, but it's a way to get you thinking about insurance because it's hard to make paying premiums funny. So try fear instead.

Think about your rioting staff trashing your business; your custard powder plant exploding causing the explosive works next door to blow up along with the adjacent fuel station. Suddenly the entire street no longer exists. If riots, fire, storms and earthquakes will not affect you much because you operate from a van, or your home, (they are insured, aren't they?) and the only gear you have is a computer or a ladder, you could self-insure (meaning you take the risk and pay the bill if the horrible happens) but some insurance, such as liability cover, may be essential.

You can't make a claim if you're not covered, so if your uninsured home and van are destroyed you are homeless and out of business. Work out the odds and consequences of it happening, which is what insurance company actuaries do as premiums are based on risk probability. If you stock explosives, which can include stuff like custard powder, premiums will be higher than if you stock bottled water.

What to insure and what self-insure depends upon what you do and the risks. If you have valuable stuff which if lost would cripple or bankrupt you, insure it. Fire and floods are common risks but liability cover is needed if you own Sky High Scaffolding or are a transplant surgeon or in any occupation where it's easy to get sued and there are truck loads of lawyers around to help. Fidelity insurance is handy if staff handle large amounts of cash or convertible documents and loss of profits or business disruption if fires or other events could stop you in your tracks. Life and/or kidnap insurance maybe handy in case of terrorism or a plane crash on the way to signing that done deal.

Consider taking voluntary excesses which means that you only claim for serious incidents as this lowers the premiums. Get quotes from two or three insurers to see how they compare, or from a broker because good brokers know the areas of specialization of insurers and can get better deals than you can. Most brokers provide good service and advice and whilst some may be tempted to over insure you, common sense can tell you if they are. Shop around and approach two or three as getting a good one can save heaps over the years. Review your insurance every year or two to see if the cover is adequate, or still needed, excesses changed and if premiums are still competitive.

Running out of money

You will be lucky if you are never short of money and unfortunate if it happens often. If you are short because you are taking too much money out of the business it can only be for a limited time before your bank or creditors force you to stop.

Even the best businesses experience financial famines when sales decline for whatever reason. How you climb out of the hole if it happens to you depends on how you got in it. If it was because of the economy, expenses will need cutting. If a rival has introduced a new products it might take awhile to combat them, but if you know your sector well it's less likely to come as a surprise.

It's easier to bite bullets if you are used to it, but try not to make it a habit. If a downturn is only temporary you will be in a better position to weather it if the cashflow has not been milked and you have a rainy-day reserve. If you need cash the fist port of call is usually your bank which may (or may not) give it to you. If they do and it covers the downturn, write a thank you letter for their files as letters of appreciation are appreciated. But if you make a habit of asking for help, writing letters is not a good idea as there will be a stack of them in your file, so thank them by phone instead.

Increasing the capital

If you can't dredge-up cash from anyone, look at increasing the share capital. You may be able to plough in extra funds from the profits you enjoyed during the good times. If you are short of cash because your business is expanding, now may be a good time to invite outsiders in. If they have the money and the right skills you could all benefit. They may want to haggle over the price and now you are on the other side of the fence you perhaps have different ideas about the value, so work out a compromise.

Overstocking

"Let's get rid of the stuff and have a cash sale." If you need cash PDQ offer 30 day credit account customers a cash discount or payment at seven days. Tell 'em you have an exciting sales

target to meet (it's true) hence this never to be repeated for a limited time offer …

Debtors and factoring

If debtors are not paying the *Credit Control* chapter helps fix it and if you think you will incur a bad debt it helps you to act before it happens.

Factor financing (factoring) by its critics is called borrowing of last resort. By its supporters it's seen as a good, if expensive, source of working capital. Points in its favour are that the factor advances 80-90% of the money owed by your debtors within days of making the sale. Then, instead of the debtor paying you they pay the factor in accordance with your normal terms of trade and when they do the factor pays you the remaining 10-20%, less a commission of 2 to 4%. This means you are giving the factor some of your gross profit. Only you can work out if it's worth it and factoring can be more expensive than borrowing money from the bank, but may be less than the merchant fees of some credit card companies.

Before the factor gives you the money they contact your customers to see if sales are genuine. Whilst you wouldn't write false invoices in order to get 90% of their value, as that would be fraud and not nice, it has happened. The factor will also tell your customer to pay them directly and not pay you as you can't have your cake and eat it.

Before deciding to factor, get a full disclosure from them and if you don't have a financial background ask an accountant - or your bank which is free. Some factoring companies are owned by banks, so ask the factor who owns them in case it's your bank as you might not get impartial advice if it does.

Besides cost other downsides of factoring can be long-term contracts, personal guarantees and recourse. Some factors want contracts of a year or more and may insist that all credit sales must be channelled through them. Shop around as not all insist on long term contracts and some will let you pick and choose which debtors to factor. Do an online search of *Factoring* to find out.

Try and avoid giving a personal guarantee and look for a factor that doesn't insist. Many want recourse (look for one that doesn't), which means if the debtor doesn't pay them they will charge your bank account with the amount advanced. You will then be hit with an unplanned withdrawal and the factor wants the personal guarantee in case the direct debit bounces. If it does and you have signed a guarantee you're in trouble. Whilst the factor will (or should have) an in-house credit control team to chase slow paying debtors, you have no control over their performance or methods. These are good reasons for refusing to give personal guarantees because, like you, the factor is in business too and should accept some of the risks of doing business.

Lawyers & accountants

Even if your business is straightforward and it's unlikely you will need legal advice, think about which lawyer to approach if things go wrong. Do though get your terms and conditions of trade up to date because that can save you more than it costs when push comes to shove with a poor-payer and for disputes.

If you are in a potentially risky sector consider appointing a lawyer at the outset. Also, do (or get) a risk assessment because if something happens you can then pick up the phone and speak to someone who knows who you are and what you do.

The same applies to accountants and if you don't have an accountant think about getting one for tax or other advice. At some stage you may have a tax audit and having an accountant can save anguish and penalties. Avoid being late with tax returns and payments because taxmen charge interest and fret, which makes them think about an audit. If you are late more than once or so or there are erratic highs, lows or refunds on your returns, you climb higher on their to-be-audited ladder.

Outsourcing

Outsourcing can be cheaper than DIY. Tasks such as payroll and bookkeeping are easy to outsource and doing so frees-up time for making a living or playing golf with customers. If you make or machine stuff, think about sub-contracting some or all of it. If you can't and you have to acquire equipment and staff, can you earn extra income by becoming an outsource specialist for other businesses that are not direct competitors; or perhaps even if they are if they trust you!

Other outsourcing advantages are that the outsource specialist becomes your creditor. Getting credit terms from them improves your cashflow and saves employment costs.

Complete the **What I can outsource** box below to see if outsourcing can reduce costs or make your business grow.

What I can outsource

What can I outsource?   Wages   YES ⬜ No ⬜

                         Bookkeeping   YES ⬜ No ⬜

                         Debtor mgt.   YES ⬜ No ⬜

                         Other admin   YES ⬜ No ⬜

                         Assembly   YES ⬜ No ⬜

                         Other   YES ⬜ No ⬜ If YES, what?

....

How can outsourcing benefit me? Better use of time ⬜ Reduce costs ⬜ Other

⬜ as below:-

....

....

Could I become an outsource specialist? YES ⬜ No ⬜ If YES list the

options ....

....

....

12_____Credit control, terms of trade and securities acts

It really was a done deal and you can't wait to get paid ...

A mega-jail would be needed today ...

You sent the invoice but the money hasn't come. After a bit of fretting you phone and are told *"we will 'pay tomorrow,"* but tomorrow never comes and neither does your money. And it probably won't unless you ask for it.

Too many businesses pay late, especially large bully-boy types. If you sell to other businesses (B2B) you probably have to sell on credit because your rivals do and that means asking customers to pay at some stage.

Never be shy to ask for your money. Credit control is quite easy, can be fun (you get paid) and without stress or damage to customer relations provided you follow basic rules, as shown in the credit control book, *Get Paid* by, err, myself. **For a preview, see Appendix 10** It's available in paperback from Amazon www.amazon.com and in the search box click ***books*** then enter ***Get Paid: How to get customers to pay.*** It is also available as a Kindle eBook from www.amazon.com/kindle and in the search box do the same as above.

With good credit control no more than 5% of your debtors should be at 60 and 90 days. Ideally *none* should but it's not a perfect world. In the getting paid game, up-to-date **Terms and Conditions of Trade** (often called *terms and conditions* or something similar) greatly help as they spell out late payment penalties and other remedies, such as dispute resolution and your maximum liability to claims. It's not necessary to shell out big bucks to a lawyer for Terms of Trade as some *legal process providers* compile quality documents for much less than what most lawyers charge. See www.terms-of-trade.com.au as an example (correct at time of writing). Get them to throw in a *Credit Account Application* form, a *Multi-purpose quotation/ estimate* form and a *Personal/directors guarantee* form too. The first two should have your Terms of Trade attached for customers to accept right from the start. This makes it hard to impossible for them to wriggle out later. The guarantee is for problem customers to put their personal money where their business mouth is if they want you to defer recovery or other action.

A quick checklist before giving credit is:

- Insist they sign your credit account application form and accept your Terms of Trade;

- Check credit references *before giving credit – do the last one first;*

- Set a credit limit of around a month to six weeks purchases and stick to it by getting them to pay if it's exceeded or they want to place further orders;

- Do professional credit checks on customers who could damage you if they defaulted. This includes existing customers who place big orders;

- Seriously consider getting personal guarantees from directors of customers who could ruin you if they default.

If signing guarantees contradicts what you read earlier, it's because there are two sides to a story and you are now on the other side. Get emotional about sticking to your guns by thinking what will happen if a customer accounting for 25% of your sales goes bust whilst owing three or more months sales. If that doesn't frighten you, make swimming with sharks a hobby.

There's an old adage that *a sale is not a sale until you get paid*. In the thrill of the chase, getting paid may only be an afterthought, but make it aforethought because it's as big a priority as the sale itself. If progress payments are standard in your industry, or a deposit with order or before repairs are undertaken then get them. If payment is on collection, get paid before releasing the goods because "Oops I have forgotten my wallet, credit card or whatever but will pop in tomorrow" might be true, but here's the problem:

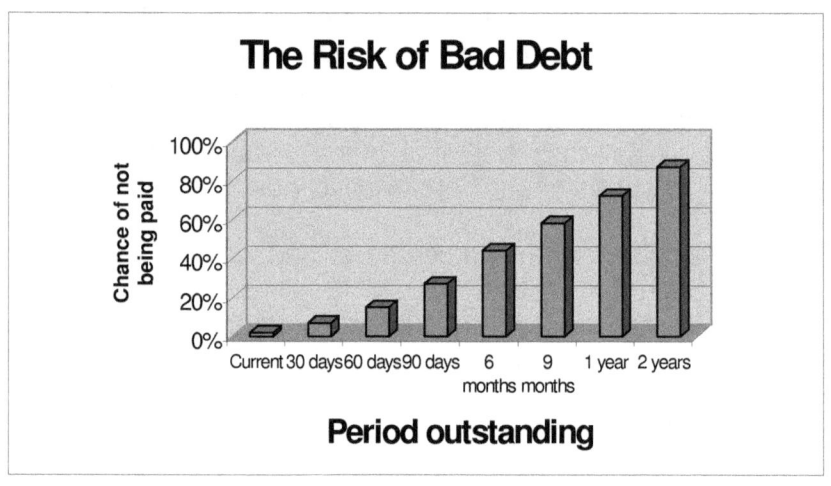

Source: American Commercial Law League

Tackle slow-payers promptly because if they are 30 days overdue you have a 7% bad debt risk. If they are 60 days late there is a 15% risk and at 90 days there is a one in four chance of never getting paid.

Good credit control rarely kills a sale - if it does you may be better off without it. If they want extra time to pay, the time to arrange that is before the sale and not when the bill's due, so if the account is large whip out the personal guarantee and your pen for them to sign it in case they can't afford one – make sure you get the pen back.

Being practical the safeguards needed when selling on credit depend on the default risk and amount involved. The *ouch-test* is a quick way of finding out. If the *ouch* will mainly be annoying and not serious, a simple check is probably all that is needed. But if not getting paid will it damage or bankrupt you contact at least three credit referrals before granting credit.

Credit control tips are In **Appendices** along with a sample Credit Account Application form. You can use it if you accept that copyright remains with the author's company and that usage is entirely at your risk.

A horse's tale - Property Securities Legislation

Australia, Canada, New Zealand and other countries have what are *called Personal Property Securities Registers* and other countries have something similar. These registers reveal who has a security interest on goods and other property. This means that what you think is yours (such as your unpaid-for goods or equipment in your customer's possession) can be seized and sold by insolvency practitioners if your customer goes broke and you won't get the stuff back or the money.

A horrible example was a $1million racehorse grazing in a trainer's paddock. The trainer became insolvent and the receiver seized and sold the horse. The horse's owner got nothing. Someone stated that "the law is an ass" (origin disputed but probably from *Revenge for Honour,* a 1654 play by English dramatist George Chapman) and the ass not only swallows-up horses it can do the same for your unpaid-for goods in your customers' premises and your equipment on construction sites. The definition of a *construction site* may include warehouses and other properties being renovated or extended, so if you are a plumber with onsite equipment and materials and the main contractor or property owner becomes insolvent you could lose your stuff. Depending where you are this may extend to your goods or equipment in your office/surgery or other rented property if the landlord becomes insolvent.

If similar laws affect you (at time of writing USA and UK do not appear to have such laws) your defence is to register a Perfected Security Interest and/or a Purchase Money Security Interest on the Personal Property Securities Register to help safeguard your ownership of what is by rights your property (but may not be not in law). If your stuff could be at risk or you own Dobbin the $1million racehorse which grazes in someone else's paddock, see your lawyer or accountant right away as such legislation is nasty and not funny.

13____Bogeymen

Is there is a problem with *your main asset*?

It's not nice being stuck in the mud so plan a how-to-get-out-of-it just in case.

I have no idea what happened to the owner of the $1million racehorse, but an out-of-the-blue event like that is likely to be catastrophic for most of us.

The best way of getting rid of bogeyman stuff is to work out the chance of the bogeyman calling, how to prevent it and what to do if he does. Tackling the not-nice before it happens is fun as it's reassuring, so think about what could cause the bogyman to call. They could be lack of money, poor management, faulty business plan (or no plan at all) and inexperience. These are not the only reasons as the loss of key assets could send you out of business, as could an insolvency practitioner seizing your equivalent of the racehorse. You could also be sued for various reasons, such as faulty workmanship which could ruin you, in which case a chunk of insurance could be handy.

Before tossing this book aside and forgetting all about owning a business, list what your bogyman risks could be over the page. Identifying those helps stop Mr Bogey calling and can identify solutions if he does.

Bogyman Risks			
	Cause	effect	solutions
Lack of customers/money			
Faulty Business plan			
No business plan			
Poor management			
Lack of experience			
Loss of crucial customers,			
Actions of competitors			
Loss/loss of use of crucial assets			
Others applicable to my business			

Some bogeyman stuff has been covered in earlier and now is the time to fill in the holes.

Loss of major asset. If your equivalent of a truck is out of action for weeks you will have no income, so either put some money aside (self insurance) or take out a loss of income insurance policy. If the asset is grazing in someone else's paddock more than a horse blanket is needed, so protect it with a *Perfected Security Interest* if applicable (see a lawyer or accountant).

Lack of cash - if you don't have any find out why. Are costs greater than the profit, are you taking too much money out or other reasons? The trip to bankruptcy starts slowly but ends quickly so act quickly to stop it using the *Bogeyman Risks* box. If you cannot increase sales then better to call it quits sooner rather than later. If inventories are too high, have a sale or do what other businesses do which is to delay paying creditors, but pay essential ones, such as the power bill and taxes. If you bought stuff on credit be cheeky and ask the salesperson for extra time to pay. Sales staff rarely have the authority for this, but they value future business and could speak nicely to their credit controller if the delay is only two or three weeks or so. If more than a month or two is needed, see the *Orderly withdrawal* and *Collapse* sections in the 'Time to go' chapter.

Other reasons for getting in the mire depend on what sort of business you have. By identifying likely causes now can provide fixes whilst you still have your wits because wits tend to vanish during crises. In the box below write the names of your bogeymen rescue team whilst and include your accountant, lawyer, insurance broker, others who could help and friendly banker. Banks like to know things in advance and most will help customers out of short-term jams. But they lose sympathy if you only tell them during the crisis and the little that's left evaporates if you don't have a plan. Write down what-if plans for events that could disrupt you, such as fire, flood, riots and loss of key employees - including yourself through illness and accidents during that nasty terrorist attack whilst signing the done-deal - a dash of insurance may be handy.

Other out-of-the blue things could be loss of customers. Losing a customer who accounts for 15% of sales could be *ouch,* but if they account for 40% it could be a disaster. Take your top four customers and if they account for more than 40% of sales compile a save-my-critical-customers plan. Write down the reasons you could lose them – they go bust, are taken over or poached by rivals and other events applicable to your business and how to recover from them or, better still, stop them from happening at all.

Many big businesses have what-if plans but few small ones do. Don't frighten yourself to death by fretting over unlikely what-ifs, but some catastrophe planning can keep you afloat if the horrible happens. Write down what could happen and who could help you overleaf.

My bogeymen and rescuers are:

If the bogeyman flies in you might have to fly by the seat of your pants, but by having a plan and contacts at least you will be wearing them when he does …

14_____Time to go

Unlike being in the forces or working for an employer, when you own a business you can call the time-to-go shot.

Long Service Medal
(Courtesy of the Australian Defence Force)

Now is a good time to plan your goodbye to the business you haven't yet started! The reason is its fun to think way ahead as it gives you a goal to make starting it even more exciting. The time to say goodbye should be before being in business changes from fun to tedium and planned ways to go are *sensible seller, pharaoh* and *tycoon*. Unfortunate ways of going are *orderly withdrawal* and *collapse*.

      The poet W. E. Henley wrote; "I am master of my fate, I am captain of my soul." Whilst the truth of this in life is questionable it can apply to business, so see if it applies to you.

Quitting time: captain, master or victim?

What are my personal goals? ....

What are my family's goals?..

How is my health? Good ❐ Some problems ❐ Don't know❐ ... if the latter see your doctor and find out

If my health is OK, how long is it likely to remain so? +10yrs ❐ + 5yrs ❐ + 2yrs ❐ - 2yrs ❐

If my health deteriorates without notice, or 'thru accident what will I do?.......................

....

....

When I quit I will: start a new business ❐ get a job ❐ retire ❐ Can I honestly do any of these? Yes ❐ No ❐ Not sure ❐

  reasons/obstacles ....

....

When is my personal mental/physical use by date likely to be? ...... years or months .....

When is my business's use by date likely to be? +10yrs ❐ + 5yrs ❐ + 2yrs ❐ -2yrs ❐ almost now ❐

If my business is expanding when will I sell? ...... years and why ....

....

....

Who shall I sell to? outsiders ❐ employees ❐ partners/directors ❐ go public ❐

If my business is performing badly, how long have I got? must close now ❐ soon be forced to ❐ still time for a controlled wind down ❐ still time to sell at a sensible price ❐ How long have I got.......... weeks/months

My other options are...

....

  Am I: a captain ❐ master ❐ victim ❐ Reasons...

....

The more successful your business is the more withdrawal options there are, but even if it's not doing too well there can be ways to exit with grace and some money.

Sensible seller

If your business is doing quite-nicely-thank-you but you no longer look forward to opening the doors on a morning and shed few tears when closing them at night, the *time-to-go* is coming. The good news is when this happens it means you are probably not a workaholic and are certainly not if you have a well-balanced life, work less than forty hours a week, take almost every weekend off, or two other days in lieu, and have regular holidays. If three days out of five are enjoyable, two are mediocre and one lousy it's time to plan your goodbye because the signs are that being in business is not as much fun anymore.

Plan your *time-to-go* right at the start to give you time to get things right, so when a buyer comes along they see a neatly run business backed up with sound accounts along with a thorough hand-over to help overcome the disagreeable reasons the buyer's accountant puts forward about your price.

By keeping your business shipshape you are a prospective seller anytime because an offer could come without notice – possibly from well-healed investors or a rival – and because everything is sound it will be saleable on a willing-buyer-willing-seller basis: the price being dictated by enjoyable negotiation and with neither of you under any pressure. Practicing what is known as *relapse prevention* in the shrink trade will keep it performing nicely and, hmm, there might just be a bit of goodwill in it for you after all.

Pharaoh

Becoming a pharaoh can set your memory in stone for generations. Imagine your image hanging from the foyer, boardroom and on fast food boxes like Colonel Saunders. But hesitate before you do it.

Before selling to outsiders, employees, other shareholders or going public becoming a pharaoh is another option. Instead of just being a picture on a fast food box, it could be your dynasty in control: your offspring and theirs and theirs for eternity. Unlike those boring pharaohs and kings, you will be alive for a while to guide your scion until your dotage and retain a shareholding to boot.

If you are the sole, or vast majority shareholder, dynasty creation could be tempting. But don't even think of it because here's a tale of two dynasties. The first became large and successful and whilst the chairman had married one of the founder's daughters, he was chairman because of ability and not because of family connections. Attempts to get jobs for the family's less talented boys and girls were nicely sidestepped and helped by dollops of dividends to reduce the temptation of killing the golden egg laying goose. This worked for three generations, but the less talented eventually came aboard and that's when the ship began to sink. The other dynasty was also large, well known and totally controlled by the founder's immediate descendants who featured in the rich list, but the dynasty totally collapsed in the next generation. This was caused by faulty decisions and inability to adapt to new conditions which could have been achieved if skilled non-family management had run the business. There are dynasties that have existed for centuries, but they are exceptions and not the rule because the rule is: rags-to-riches-to-rags in three generations. Sometimes it takes less and other times more, so if you have talented boys and girls, will the next generations be talented? Playing intergenerational pharaoh can ultimately mummify a business.

If being pharaoh no longer seems a good idea then take professional advice from a Business Succession Planner. Larger firms of accountants and lawyers have departments dedicated to this but if your business is a success the steep fees can be worth it.

Tycoon

You started with a few tools in a garden shed and now have lots of staff, a huge factory and increasing profits. Well done and now you are on the guest list of the rich and famous, so get out there and enjoy it. Now you have piles of money, use some of it for charitable purposes. If you've got lots doing that can be a job in itself.

Happy workers lining up to cheer you

If you like what you are doing and don't want to enjoy yourself by spending a bit of your fortune, by all means stay working, but reduce your hours by delegating to the bright sparks you hired because unless you do they will leave. Besides, your company may grow faster as a result.

If you are healthy success gives you heaps of options; such as selling some or all of your shares, selling to other directors, shareholders, your rivals or going public. But having lots of options is *the problem* and stops many successful people from making a decision because making it is not as simple as it sounds. How sad!

If getting out of business could be a problem see a business succession planner as mentioned at the end of the *Pharaoh* section – hang the fees, you can afford them and your finance director may class them as a business expense, which in some ways they are. Even if you have clear ideas on how to exit, it may be wise to see a Succession Planner to avoid mistakes or friction with colleagues or family if they work in the business or own shares.

Some of the well-healed have set up charitable trusts and donated a big proportion of their wealth to it. Examples include Mr & Mrs Gates, Mr Trump and others. An earlier example was the British car making tycoon, Lord Nuffield, who intriguingly said *that giving the money away was harder than making it.*

If you have more money than you and your family need then why not do the same as those other successful people? There is a great need and great good can be done. Christians are encouraged to tithe (it means giving 10% of your earnings to God) and if you are a Christian why not do it with your fortune too? It doesn't have to be a tithe and can be greater or less than 10%. Most church donations are used wisely, but priests and bishops are often not well schooled in money management, so if the amount is large use your savvy to help them use it wisely, perhaps using the Parable of the Talents as a guide. If this means being involved in how the funds are spent you have probably found the most enjoyable and responsible job you've ever had!

It's beyond the scope of this book to go any further on how the rich can use their time and money. But even if you are not yet rich, planning how to best use your wealth in anticipation being rich can stimulate you to start your own business (or buy into one) and make your fortune. When you do, use it and your time wisely and everyone will be better off for it, especially you.

Orderly withdrawal

Now to unfortunate reasons for getting out of business before going out of business.

Dunkirk 1940 was a bit rough but it came right in the end

Good plans help prevent disasters but even the best plans go wrong – the British and French didn't think the Germans would attack like they did in 1940, so if your plan hasn't worked (or you didn't plan because you knew window cleaning inside out) see if you can avoid turning defeat into a rout.

Find out the reason(s) for the setback. Could the business do better if you were no longer there? If that may be so, is there someone who could run it, such as a new owner or even a competitor? You might not get a lot but if you have something valuable it may be saleable. Identify what will make your business hum and why you haven't been able to accomplish it. As you will probably be in hoc to a bank, see if they will give you a few months to find a buyer, or someone to run it. There has been lots of bad publicity about banks and giving you time to sort things out might save them from more of it. If they don't agree, gently hinting about publicity and suggesting that by foreclosing they might not get all their money back (especially if you have not pledged your home as discussed in the *Raising the cash* chapter)) may persuade the banker, and their manager, to cover their backsides by giving you more time. But only buy time if you really can use it to reduce your losses and if all that buying time will do is to increase your losses, get out straightaway.

If the horrible looks like happening keep this book handy because what you wrote in the *Bogeymen* chapter can help you out. Discuss all options with your family or confidants as they might be able to see the wood-from-the-trees better than you. If your business is salvageable and the main things that are wrong are lack of money or a few bad decisions (or bad debts), you might still be able to sell it as a going concern. You could then recover more than you would by selling assets piecemeal unless they are expensive ones that are worth more than the business is.

Collapse

It's falling apart and you want to run away to avoid paying your debts. People do run away from businesses without telling their creditors or bank and whilst some, especially banks, may get them eventually other creditors give up after awhile.

A bankruptcy or winding-up notice may arrive or a debenture holder appoints an administrator, receiver or liquidator. Such folk can pitch up unannounced to seize the assets - if there are any - before someone else does.

This section is not to aid and abet those wanting to default on their debts but most receivers of small businesses soon give up as they prefer tidy jobs, payment of their fees and a big enough return to their masters to get more business. One receiver wrote to unsecured creditors saying that following a successful receivership (success = 100% payment to the debenture holder and payment of the receivership fees) there was no money left for anybody else and the company would be liquidated.

Unless there is a debenture a receiver cannot be appointed, but a liquidator can. The bank is the main worry and it's hard to talk them out of using their trusty recovery methods, so look for loopholes. Was the paperwork properly signed and initialled in front of witnesses? Did your spouse or other parties sign at the same time, was it all explained to them, were you sane at the time or was it signed under duress? Even if there is only a tiny chink, exploit it for all it's worth because a court just might agree with you. Do it face-to-face as the possibility of a chink may be revealed by a worried look whilst they eye their paperwork. If they do, start negotiating. You have nothing to lose by offering partial settlement – make it low if you twig their paperwork really is defective. Unless you are very certain their security is not worth the paper it's printed on, offer a face-saver otherwise they will go for you. If you have become a connoisseur of bankers as mentioned in the *Raising the cash* chapter you will have experience of what bankers are like. Without being dishonest do the same with creditors. Were the goods/services of good quality because if your current state is their fault you may have a case against them.

To salvage more, try to wind the business down instead of walking away and risking being hunted down, so keep your integrity and pay back as much as possible. Finally, if someone else's business collapses and they ask you for mercy, have a heart. If something's wrong with your paperwork, or they have a dispute, you could lose anyway.

15_____To do or not to do?

William Shakespeare 1564 to 1616

To be, or not to be: that is the question:
Whether 'tis nobler in the mind to suffer
The slings and arrows of outrageous fortune,
Or to take arms against a sea of troubles,
And by opposing end them?
(From William Shakespeare's play, Hamlet)

"To do or not to do" is a question only you can answer about starting a business, or buying one, or into one. But if you have got this far you probably know what the answer is. If it's a strong *yes*, you now have a lot of tools to work out how to do it, how profitable it could be and when and how to say goodbye.

If going into business is not for you - or you or your spouse have a gut-feel that it's not right as shown in Chapters 1, 2 and 3, then don't do it. But to avoid future *if-only* attacks, look at the reasons again and if they are sound, write them down to inoculate yourself against *if-only* attacks if you get them, which you probably won't because you have made a decision based on sound reasoning. If leaping is not for you, don't leap.

If the reasons for delaying going into business could disappear in future it's only a timing issue that is stopping you and provided you are healthy there is no age restriction on going into many kinds of business. Whilst manual work needs youthful strength and some other sectors seem to be the domain of younger people, experience coupled with knowledge out-trumps youthfulness any day of the week. Examples proving this include the collapses of talent-bedecked Enron and Long Term Capital Management - the latter had Nobel Prize winners on its staff and both were at the time about the biggest failures in commercial history. Remember what Jefferson said about the ploughman and the professor!

I hope this book will help you create a successful business which gives you fun and profits for years to come. If you believe you can do it, go for it with all your heart, with all your mind and with all your strength. And start right now – some of the stuff in the appendices may save you a bit of money.

Appendices

To help you on the way

and perhaps save you money

Telemarketing

The success of telemarketing depends on the telemarketer's skill, the script, your offer, the quality of the telemarketing database and timing.

If using a bureau insist they use people experienced in your field. If they have no one but say their staff are quick learners you will be paying for their learning. If you engage a freelancer, tell them what your business is about and what your objectives are - seems obvious but you would be surprised about how vague some telemarketing bureau customers are. Try and offer an incentive, such as commission for leads that result in sales.

Scripts are best designed by those who know how to do them and a freelancer or bureau may be able to do it, but you must provide the input and vet their script. Len's Laundry's script is:

"Hi I am Mary from Len's Laundry. Can I speak to your washing manager please?"

If they have nothing to wash, the wrong database is being used and Mary's time and Len's money are wasted. When getting through to the washing manager, Mary says:

"Hello, I am Mary from Len's Laundry and we provide sparkling overalls that are washed and ironed so they look and feel new. We offer a free mending service for the first month and have a free collection and delivery service. Would you like to know more?"

If they are keen (or sort-of) Mary gets their contact details and asks if Len can phone them. Before saying goodbye, Mary says:

"Can you tell me who currently does your laundering?" to see if it's in-house or Wendy's Washing and if it is another launderer she says: **"Do they offer a free mending service or anything special?"** She records that too.

If you can't get a decent telemarketing database you might have to rent one and if you don't know where to find one, do a search for *direct marketing services* (or similar). Bureaus usually have databases but you don't know how good they are and whilst they might not have been used by your competitors they will have been used for other clients, so contact some of their clients to see how satisfied they were. If the bureau won't let you, go elsewhere. If you decide to proceed ask to see their database to check that it is suitable.

Timing of calls affects response rates. You are paying for their time, so insist calls are made at times appropriate to your business - if possible, check they actually do so. Telemarketing is hit-and-miss with lots of calls for a small number of successes. If you use a bureau, limit your first trial to five hours or a maximum of ten and if it fails discontinue it. Some bureaus are so aware of their limitations they try and tie you to contracts first. As a carrot they might offer to do the script free of charge, but even then limit it to a short-term trial. If they really are good they shouldn't object, should they?

Buying a business – questions to ask

Notice: This is only a guide to basic checks before buying a business or a franchise. It can assist in helping to make a *I-won't-buy* decision but is not comprehensive enough for a *I-will* decision and is not a substitute for professional advice.

If the vendor or their agent think you are serious, bits of paper will start wafting towards you, but before signing anything take professional advice unless you are knowledgeable on the contents of the bits of paper. Even then, run it past a colleague in case you have missed something serious.

The story of another buyer being out there might pop up now and if it does you can be sure of one thing: that is the offer, if it exists, is not high enough. There is unlikely to be any other valid reason for it not being accepted and tales that you are the 'preferred buyer' don't wash even if it's a laundry. There may be another buyer but their offer might not have been accepted because the vendor wants to crank the price up, and wants you to be the crank to do it.

Next comes the little matter of what part of the business are you buying. Is it the assets or the company? Advisors usually recommend buying the assets and not the company because you don't know what the liabilities are, and perhaps neither does the vendor. If you have to buy the company for whatever reason ensure that the vendor signs a full disclosure and personal liability indemnities drawn up by your lawyer, but because of family trusts and other barriers, these might not be worth the paper they are printed on.

If you are buying into the business ensure the other shareholders and directors sign a full disclosure of potential liabilities and indemnify you for claims against the company for events occurring prior to you buying in. Even if you are buying the business from a sole trader, full disclosures and indemnities should be obtained as whilst you might not be liable for previous debts you could, in practice, have to rectify defective work or replace defective goods. If it is a straightforward business, such as window cleaning or lawn mowing, this might not be an issue because the amount of repeat business can tell you if customers are satisfied, as should the accounts or turnover figures, but if turnover is dropping look closely at the reasons. If turnover is increasing check that it is likely to continue after you buy it.

Look at the accounts. If they require a confidentiality agreement read it carefully and strike out anything unreasonable; such as restrictions preventing you from looking at other businesses, or a restraint of trade clause that could hinder or prevent you from starting your own business. Onerous clauses are unusual but not unheard of and extreme ones try to stop people from using even general knowledge in anyway apart from buying that business, so if it feels fishy get legal advice before signing.

Perfect accounts

After the niceties you might be given a nice set of accounts: income and expenses, balance sheet with historical comparisons, source and application of funds and forecasts. When you become really serious, full supporting schedules will be provided with bank reconciliations and debtor lists showing that the sales are genuine, creditors are paid on time, there are no contingent liabilities and all your questions satisfactorily answered. If you are skilled in the art of reading accounts you will be delighted, or if accounts are not your forte, your accountant will be impressed.

Not-so-perfect accounts

Now to reality. The accounts are not up to date. The few records they have are dubious, *"we are sorting it out and will soon be there."* Scraps of paper are produced, but nothing really supports their little gold mine claim. Instead, there are knowing winks about cash jobs and revenue is, well, not totally declared to the taxman and you will benefit from this too, so buy quickly. If they own a shiny Ferrari and luxury boat and you currently work for the tax office, you now know who to audit.

There may be reasons for accounts being behind, but if the vendor is serious about selling there is no valid excuse for them being unavailable. Even if they are not models of ideal accounting standards, they should at least show sales, expenses, profits, assets and liabilities and supported by information to check them. If they need time to get them up to date insist they do so before making an offer. Or, make it conditional that everything they have told you is accurate and the offer will only be valid when you are satisfied it is.

Are the books cooked?

By starting a business you won't need to see if the books are cooked. Finding out is costly unless you are experienced enough to DIY – even then be careful and get a second opinion. Even if the books accurately show the state of the business, the assets, liabilities and contingencies need checking. This isn't necessary if you start your own business because there won't be any! The accuracy of forecasts, budgets, cashflow and everything else needs verifying in both cases, but professional fees can be higher when buying a business because there are more things to check. For some sectors there are financial performance indicators and good accountants use them as comparisons. The bright side of buying a business is it will have customers (if not, what are you buying?) whereas a new one will not.

Stuff to look at

The **balance sheet** shows what the assets and liabilities are. **Assets** include inventory, equipment, vehicles, debtors and everything else you are buying. But take the value of intangibles with a pinch of salt. Intangibles are things that do not physically exist, except on paper, such as goodwill ('badwill' rarely appears in accounts but can exist), intellectual property, trade marks, brands and anything else you cannot cuddle or hit with a hammer. A lot of creative accounting has occurred using intangibles to tart-up balance sheets by inserting stuff you can't cuddle or bash, so why buy them? Bumf such as, *"these are accepted commercial and accounting practices,"* are only acceptable if they are valuable to you. Now, what does all this say about buying a business is safer than starting one?

Liabilities include amounts owing to creditors, banks, lease companies, tax and all other claims on the business. The risk is they may not all be shown, which is another reason why buying the assets instead of the company is safer. Deducting the assets from the liabilities shows whether the company is solvent. If assets exceed liabilities then it is sort-of solvent. But the acid test is: can it pay its bills as and when they fall due? To see if it can, add up the current assets (cash, bank balances, debtors and ignore things that cannot quickly be converted to cash, especially intangibles) then deduct current liabilities (creditors, overdraft and other current debts). If current assets exceed current liabilities then it is reasonably solvent. But if current liabilities exceed current assets it is technically insolvent and will have cashflow problems that could blow it apart. Share capital is also a liability but ignore it for the moment because shareholders are last on the list to get paid if it goes belly-up.

Income and expenditure accounts show sales, expenses and the profit, or loss, with previous year's figures shown as a comparison. Things to look at are:

Sales (also called *turnover,* or if fiddled, *churnover*). If the business has been going a long time, look at the trend for at least three years and ideally the last five or more to see if sales are going up or down and why. If sales are steadily increasing it indicates the business is flourishing, but is not total proof, so ask to see the GST/tax returns (when you become very serious your accountant should carefully check that everything is genuine) because very few businesses overstate income and pay more tax than needed! Another risk with turnover is product mix. If one product accounts for a big portion of sales and demand for it drops there is a problem.

Expenses are the costs of running the business, such as wages, rents, vehicle running costs, power, repairs, depreciation, bad debts, advertising, stationery, interest and all other costs. To make the business look better the seller might write-back personal items charged as business expenses and if so the tax office will be intrigued. They can't have their cake and eat it, so ignore the write-backs and it serves them right for cheating.

Don't necessarily run away from a loss making business if you can pick it up cheap, which is great if you can make it profitable. The industry average is an indicator and if you know the industry well you would know what can be done. There may be reasons to increase the profits of a business by eliminating some expenses but ignore restatement of profits to crank up the price because it's what they told the taxman that counts.

Your business name in full ("the Company")
CREDIT ACCOUNT APPLICATION

Legal name of business _____ Date established _____

Trading name if different _____

Street & postal address (if different) _____

Delivery address (if different) _____

Registered office address (if different) _____

Phone _____ Mobile _____ Fax_____ E-mail _____

Bank and Branch _____ Accountants _____

Solicitor _____

Are you a (please) Company   Partnership   Sole Trader   Other   (i.e. Trust, Charity
If you are a Sole Trader/Partnership details of nearest relative not living with you:

Name of relative _____Relationship_____

Address of relative _____
Details of (as applicable)**: Directors, partners, trustees or other principals**

1. Full name _____ Phone number _____

Residential address _____

2. Full name _____ Phone number _____

Residential address _____

3. Full name _____ Phone number _____

Residential address _____
(Please list on separate sheet if more than three)

Amount of credit required per month $_____ If you are a company, paid up capital is _____

Who do we contact in your business for:
 Buying/authorising orders_____ Paying accounts _____
Their email addresses are _____
Trade References

1. Name _____ Phone No _____

2. Name _____ Phone No _____

3. Name _____ Phone No _____

4. Name _____ Phone No _____

I/we agree to fully accept and abide by the Company's Terms and Conditions of Trade contained herein and as may be amended from time to time. I/we hereby acknowledge that ownership of all goods and/or services supplied to us remains with the Company until all moneys outstanding have been paid in full and all obligations have been met. We agree not to lodge any security interests in the Company's goods/services or permit any other parties to lodge any security interests in the Company's goods/services under the Personal Property Securities Act or on any other register, charge document or instrument until all our obligations to the Company have been fulfilled. I/we authorize any person, organization or company to provide the Company with any information that may be required at any time regarding this application and my/our credit worthiness.

Applicants name _____ Position_____

Applicant's signature _____ Date _____

Business-to-business (B2B) credit checking only (not suitable for personal credit applications)

A simple credit check can be enough if the main damage a default would do is the annoyance of losing a small sum of money. Get customers to complete the Credit Account Application form, including trade references. Most forms only ask for three references but ours asks for four because skilful slow payers pay two or three creditors on time and use them as credit references, but few such types pay four on time.

Phone the fourth referee first and ask: "do they pay their account more or less on time?" This tells you most things you need to know and you learn if they are good, fair or bad payers, but even if they appear to be good payers phone at least two others before granting credit.

Avoid giving credit to individuals as credit checks are harder and also they may be one-off customers and paying you might not be a priority. If you are, say, a plumber fixing a householder's leak, getting paid on the spot may not be possible, but invoice them promptly and stamp/ write in red 'payment by return please'.

Look at alternatives to credit, such as cash, EFT and credit cards (some businesses add the card commission to the bill). If you sell to trades-people, discounts are best as they are hard to contact in working hours - they could be on a roof and when they go home paying you may not be much of a priority.

Accepting cheques is the last option because they can bounce and you might not know about it for a week.

An increasing problem with getting credit references is privacy legislation which can extend to B2B credit checks. Whilst the credit application form includes a clause giving you permission to check their credit worthiness, some businesses are reluctant to help. If you encounter this, simply say to a senior manager "Surely you also do credit checks on new customers, don't you?"

Credit control methods

The object of credit control is to get paid without upsetting your customers or yourself. Phoning still remains the quickest and most effective way of getting paid, but some people find this hard to do. Other methods include faxing, which works for B2B debtors provided the debtor has a fax, emailing or even writing but that's out of fashion and takes too long. To help, buy my book, **Get Paid** as shown further on.

Notice. The following is an example only and it is not a legal document. Seeing a lawyer is recommended for all legal documents and advice. If this example is used it is entirely at the users risk.

CONFIDENTIALITY AGREEMENT IN FAVOUR OF:
(Your business's name here) and their heirs, successors and/or assigns
[Hereinafter referred to as "the Business"]

MA0DE BY: (Insert the other person(s) full name(s) and address(s)
[Hereinafter referred to as "the Interested Party"]

I/we the Interested Party hereby agree:

1. To keep all information provided by the Business totally confidential and to use it for the sole purpose of purchasing of (insert what it is) hereafter called "the Purpose" and for no other purposes whatsoever;

2. Not to copy or otherwise utilize any part of the Confidential Information except as may be reasonably necessary for the Purpose and that any copies made shall be the property of the Business;

3. Not to disclose the Confidential Information to third parties or to its employees except to such third parties or its employees who need to have access to the Confidential Information for the sole reason of the Purpose;

4. To be responsible for the performance of Clauses 1, 2, 3 and 4 above on the part of its employees or third parties to whom the Confidential Information is disclosed to;

5. Return of Information. Upon request of the Business the Interested Party shall immediately return all documents and materials (and all copies thereof) containing the Confidential Information and to certify that it has complied with this agreement;

6. The undertakings in Clauses 1 to 6 continue notwithstanding completion of the Purpose and the Interested Party shall continue to be bound by the undertakings set out herein;

7. Should any part of this agreement be invalid for any reason then any such part shall be deleted without affecting the validity of the remaining portions of this agreement.

8. Governing Law. This agreement shall be governed by the Laws of (insert the country and/or state and preferably the town where you want to take out proceedings).

Signed by the Interested Party this .... Day of .... 20..

....
Full Name (Print)   Signature

Contents are on next page. **Buy paperback or Kindle version at:** http://www.amazon.com/Get-Paid-How-get-customers/dp/1451550650/ref=sr_1_56?s=books&ie=UTF8&qid=1377039308&sr=1-56&keywords=Get+Paid!+-+the+book

To buy the Kindle issue visit
http://www.amazon.com/dp/B004HO5FLE

Contents

ISBN: 1451550650
ISBN-13: 9781451550658

If you have got this far congratulations because you are now well on the way to owning a business – unless you have thumbed through the book's contents before buying it. If so and you really want to start a business, or buy one, then first buy **Your Business Your Future?** to get you on your way.

I wish you the very best and if you decide to go ahead, make it fun and let the fun continue until it's time for you to sell your soon-to-be business …

THE END

or is it the start of …

Your Business

Your Future?

If you (or friend) want the Kindle version
the Kindle book number is B013VZGI2O

www.ingramcontent.com/pod-product-compliance
Lightning Source LLC
Chambersburg PA
CBHW051921170526
45168CB00001B/486